# THEY CALLED IT HOME

# THEY CALLED IT HOME

## Santa Cruz, California

## Margaret Koch

1974

**VALLEY PUBLISHERS**

Fresno, California

International Standard Book Number 0-913548-27-8

Printed in the United States of America

# About These Houses . . .

The first — very first — houses in the area that was to become Santa Cruz County, were shelters of tree branches and leaves.

The Ohlone Indians thrust the ends of long branches into the earth in a circle, then bent the tops over and secured them. These temporary shelters were handy because when the interior insect population got too large for comfort, the brush shelter could be burned and a new one erected.

The second houses to be constructed in the Santa Cruz area were the adobes of Santa Cruz Mission days. Only one adobe of the original Mission compound remains — and it is a rarity, a duplex, the School Street Adobe. Foundations for the adobes were usually limestone or sandstone rocks. The adobe bricks started about three feet up the walls, off the earth. Roofs were tile, bent over the Indian workmen's thighs, and baked in the sun.

In the 1850's, with the influx of Yankees from New England, Santa Cruz got its first kiln-baked brick buildings and its first New England-type wood houses.

Two of these very early brick buildings remain. The Flatiron Building, so-called because of its triangular shape, sits at the junction of Pacific Avenue with Front Street, at the Lower Plaza.

The Leslie Building sits at the top of Mission Hill at the entrance to the City Schools Offices. It has been plastered over, its windows reshaped, and is hardly recognizable today as the town's first brick building.

Both the Flatiron and Leslie Buildings had iron shutters in the early days, and the Flatiron had bullet pockmarks as well, from the bandit Tiburcio Vasquez's memorable visit to town in 1872.

The Leslie Building was constructed when Santa Cruz Mission Plaza was the main center of the business district. When the center of town moved down on the "flat" several years later, the brick Leslie store was left high and dry.

The 1860's and 1870's brought the handsome *Italianate Style* to the Santa Cruz area. It is characterized by small front porticoes, slanted bay windows and thin columns that sometimes extend up to enclose second floor windows. Roofs are sometimes flat. Usually there are quoins, or wood blocks imitating stone, placed at the corners of these houses.

*Victorian Gothic*, popular in the same years, features pointed archways and elaborately carved boards beneath the eaves, referred to as "barge" or "verge" boards. It also can be identified by its split pillars.

*Mansard Style*, also called Second Empire Style from Napoleon III, was much built in the 1860's. It is characterized by a steeply slanting roof that permits space for a full extra floor, and dormer windows in the top floor.

*Eastlake Style*, of which Santa Cruz has a wealth of fine examples, came in the later 1800's. Eastlakes were usually referred to as "villas." They were always embellished with gingerbread, towers, arches, and they have been described as "squarish, notched and jutting." The Eastlake style is named for Sir Charles Locke Eastlake of England who wrote, in 1868, *Hints on Household Taste.*

*Stick Style* was also popular in this period, and again, Santa Cruz has a wealth of it, mixed with Eastlake, with Gothic, with Queen Anne and just about everything else. "Stick" is so-called because it features sticks nailed on top of sticks to form ornate decorations, such as sunbursts and other flights of carpenters' fancy.

*Queen Anne*, from 1890 to 1900 mainly, was an English import. Late Victorian, heavy on ornamentation, it took fishscale shingles and conical towers as its particular hallmark. Stained glass windows, latticed doorways, fine woodwork and entry halls with notable staircases were also of this period. Queen Anne was sometimes built of stone or brick, although Santa Cruz Queen Annes are of redwood.

*Octagonals* and *Orientals* were popular in the United States in the 1850's but are rare today. Santa Cruz' famed octagonal, the former County Hall of Records, was built of brick in 1882.

*Mission Revival* style was popular from 1900 to 1910 with towers, arched belfries, domes, and the Espadana, that graceful facade. A raised gable of curves and squares, it may best be seen in Santa Cruz on Piedmont Court.

*Colonial Revival* was much admired about 1890 and was classical in appearance with hipped roof, pilasters and pillars. Often there was a Palladian window or colonnaded front porch.

And then there were the many simple wood houses with spindle work on their porches or up under their eaves, perhaps a bit of "stick work" somewhere, or a single curved bay window in lieu of a Queen Anne tower. There is no particular period name for these humbler homes of which Santa Cruz has more than any other type...Descriptions range from "Victorian" to "Carpenter's Bastard." However, these were the homes in which the majority of Santa Cruz County citizens lived, loved, married, raised their children, and from which they were buried. They were not the height of elegance — but they served admirably.

## About the Artists . . .

### HULDA HOOVER McLEAN

Hulda Hoover McLean attended McGill University in Canada and Stanford University at Palo Alto, graduating with degrees in psychology and political science. She is the daughter of the late Theodore J. Hoover who was Dean of the School of Engineering at Stanford. He visited Santa Cruz County in 1898 as a student, was greatly impressed with a canyon and valley on the northern border of the county, returned in 1912 and purchased the property. Mrs. McLean and her husband, who have three sons, have made their home at Rancho del Oso for the past 25 years.

Hulda has written a reminiscent biography of her uncle, the late President Herbert Hoover, which is to be published this summer by Stanford University.

She is working on a book of shells of northern Santa Cruz County beaches and is illustrating it with her pen and ink drawings. She served as supervisor of Seaside District, Santa Cruz County, for six years, and wrote an analytical book on county government which is still in demand as a guide.

Her pen and ink drawings:

| | |
|---|---|
| *Smith House* | *The New Baldwin House* |
| *Halsey House* | *Weeks House* |
| *School Street Adobe* | *Palais Monte Carlo* |
| *Santa Cruz Mission* | *Triplett House* |
| *Martha Wilson House* | *Scottish Castle* |
| *Alice's House* | *The Octagonal Gem* |

*Soquel Congregational Church*

### STANTON POWERS

Stanton Powers, who is responsible for five of the pen and ink drawings of houses, makes his home in Aptos, Santa Cruz County.

He is a graduate of San Jose State University where he also earned his master's degree in art. His work has been shown at Christie's in London, Left Bank Galleries in Paris, Huntington Hartford Museum of Modern Art in New York City, and Pan's Gallery in Beverly Hills.

His work also is in the private collections of Truman Capote, Vincent Price, Liberace and the late Edward G. Robinson.

His pen and inks are:
*The Breakers*
*Cliff Crest*
*Hagemann House* [*Live Oak Ranch*]
*Bay View Hotel*
*Cooper House*

### DONI TUNHEIM

Doni (Mrs. Edward) Tunheim was born in Bakersfield and earned a B.A. in art at San Jose State University. She moved to Santa Cruz with her husband in 1962 and at once was attracted to the city's Victorian homes. The Tunheims bought one of the historic structures — Sadler House — and are gradually and carefully restoring certain portions of it. They have two small sons. Doni is a freelance designer and an active member of Santa Cruz Historical Society.

Her work:
*Sadler House* (pen and ink)

### CYNTHIA MATHEWS

Cynthia Mathews grew up in Oakland and Berkeley. With family roots in that area on both sides of her family, she developed an early interest in local history, and a particular fascination with the area's old houses.

She studied at Pomona College and the University of California at Berkeley, a third generation graduate, with a minor in art. In 1970 she moved with her husband and two children to Santa Cruz where they have become owners of a Victorian house themselves. She continues to teach and do a variety of freelance art work.

Her work:
*Haslam House* (pen and ink)

## ROY RYDELL

Roy Rydell is a native of Minneapolis, Minnesota, but came to Los Angeles with his parents at age 13. He attended Chouinard Art Institute and graduated from University of Southern California in 1937 with a degree in fine arts. Going to Europe, he studied at Atelier 17 and Academie de la Grande Chaumiere in Paris. He has designed jewelry, furniture and interiors and is a licensed landscape architect with the State of California. He and his wife came to Santa Cruz in 1947 and after several years, purchased the old Ocean View Schoolhouse at Bonny Doon which they converted into their home. Roy Rydell is president of Santa Cruz Historical Society and co-authored a recent book on garden design for Sunset Publishers.

His work:
*The Ornament to the Corner*, which is his own building.

## About the Photographers . . .

All the new photographs in this book are the work of two men: Pete Amos and Bill Lovejoy.

Pete Amos, chief photographer for *The Santa Cruz Sentinel* newspaper, was born in a Victorian house on Stanford Avenue in Santa Cruz, the fifth son of Earl and Helen Amos. He attended Santa Cruz schools, graduating from high school in 1952, then enlisting in the U.S. Navy. He did public relations work on a tour of Europe, and tracked missiles from jet planes at Point Mugu in California. He left the Navy in 1956 and started covering photo assignments for the Santa Cruz newspaper at that time. He is married, and he and his wife Louise have four children. Pete is presently building his own small airplane in his spare time.

Bill Lovejoy, also a native of Santa Cruz, son of Walt and Violet Lovejoy, graduated from Santa Cruz High in 1968. While in high school Bill started working part-time with *The Santa Cruz Sentinel* sports department. When he completed his third year at San Jose State University, he came to work full time, joining the newspaper photo staff in May of 1971.

# Table of Contents

## SECTION III: SUCCESS STORIES, OLD AND NEW *continued*

## SECTION IV: OUT OF TOWN...

Section I

# Gone: Some of the Architectural Glories of Yesteryear

# Cherry Court

When Alfred Hinds built a fine new home for his family at the junction of Church and Chestnut Streets, Duncan McPherson decided he had to do likewise. Duncan's wife was the former Amelia Hinds, Alfred's sister.

In a way, it was a friendly family rivalry. Alfred Hinds was a prominent businessman; Duncan McPherson was editor and publisher of the town's main newspaper, *The Santa Cruz Sentinel.*

The Hinds had eight children, four of whom perished in the diphtheria epidemic of 1876. The McPhersons had nine children, five of whom lived to adulthood. Big houses were practical in those days: help was cheap; families were big.

When Alfred, a busy realtor, had his imposing home constructed, it was something of a showplace in Santa Cruz. In the early 1890's brother-in-law McPherson decided to go him one better with Cherry Court.

The area of Church, Chestnut, Walnut, Lincoln and Center Streets was one of orchards, and Duncan McPherson had his home built near the corner of Chestnut and Church Streets, in the midst of a cherry orchard. A circular drive entered on one street, curved around the mansion and departed by way of the other street. In spring the delicate blossoms surrounded the house with clouds of faint fragrance. In summer the fruits hung red and juicy, attracting every boy and bird in the town.

Cherry Court was enormous, with a basement, two stories above ground, plus an attic, imposing front entrance steps, peaks over bay windows and much wood trim. It had 20 rooms, including a billiard room, two parlors, library, solarium, pantry, main kitchen, a canning kitchen, bedrooms for the family and for the help. It cost $10,500 — a fabulous amount in that day.

In the back was a huge barn that held several buggies, a carriage or two, maybe a surrey. Three or four horses were also on hand to power the wheels.

Cherry Court was a castle within itself. In the cool cellar there were shelves of canned fruits and vegetables, pickles and preserves. Crocks of meat put down in lard stood fast against a hungry day. Upstairs in the storage pantry pies and cheeses perfumed the air.

The McPherson family lived well, and not only from a culinary viewpoint. In one parlor there were a pump organ and a piano. The library held hundreds of books. When ladies of the First Congregational Church came to call they might enjoy an afternoon musicale, or a poetry reading.

The family lived in the huge old house for about 20 years, through the turn of the century and into a new age where "hired girls" were not so easy to come by. Amelia and Duncan were getting older too, and their social lives were slowing down. They didn't need such a large home.

In the early 1920's they sold Cherry Court to a local contractor, Darrow Palmer. It was used as a rooming house for a brief time, then was torn down to make way for a modern office building.

By that time the cherry orchards had vanished too. Houses stood elbow to elbow on streets that had been paths or lanes, when Cherry Court was built in the 1890's.

*One of the finest Eastlake houses in Santa Cruz, with stick style detailing, this house was demolished in the 1920's.*

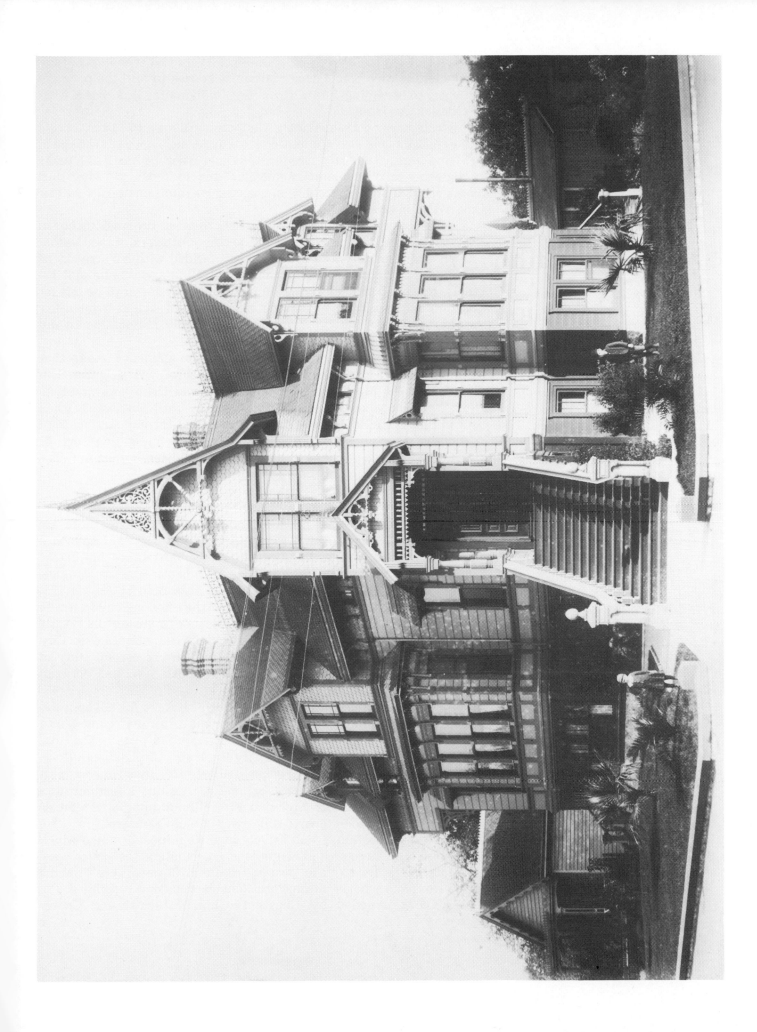

# The Hihn Mansion

It's a long way from eating manzanita berries to still the pangs of hunger, to becoming Santa Cruz' first millionaire. But that's what Frederick A. Hihn did.

He was born in Holzminden, Germany, August 16, 1829, one of nine children, and was apprenticed to a mercantile house at the age of 15. Apparently he didn't care for it because when he heard of a party emigrating to Wisconsin he made plans to join it; shortly after this, news of the California gold rush changed his mind and he set sail for the West instead.

On October 12, 1849, his ship, the brig *Reform*, dropped anchor in San Francisco Bay and Hihn set out for the south fork of the Feather River. Unfortunately, the winter rains coincided with his arrival, the river rose to flood stage and washed out Hihn's workings and his tools. He found himself living on manzanita berries until he left for Sacramento and a job — making candy. He did well at it for a few weeks, until the American River flooded its banks at Sacramento and destroyed the candy factory.

After another brief try at the mines, Hihn gained a stake that allowed him to buy two hotels in Sacramento — the Uncle Sam House and the Mechanics' Exchange. He sold them and moved to San Francisco where he operated a drugstore until May, 1851, when one of San Francisco's devastating fires roared through and left him penniless. Discouraged completely, he was planning to return to Germany when he passed a friend who also had been burned out. The friend was shoveling hot coals out of the way.

"What are you doing?" Hihn asked.

"Getting ready to build my business again."

Hihn turned this over in his mind and decided to try once more. He entered a partnership, came to Santa Cruz in 1851, and opened a mercantile store on Pacific Avenue. When hard times hit in the 1850's, Hihn bartered his store goods for wheat, lumber, shingles, butter, eggs — practically anything — and grew rich.

He married Therese Paggen in 1853 and they had six children who lived to adulthood. In 1872 he built his fine mansion on Locust Street, the house which in later years would become Santa Cruz City Hall. But before he built it, the Hihns lived in the second story of their mercantile business, located on Pacific Avenue, between Mission and Locust Street.

Hihn became a real estate operator, with "Homes for a Thousand Families" as his motto. He was instrumental in developing Santa Cruz' first city water supply. He built the railroad from Santa Cruz to Watsonville. He organized the City Bank and City Savings Bank of Santa Cruz. He served as a school trustee, a county supervisor, a state assemblyman, and one of Santa Cruz County's leading lumbermen. There was hardly a pie that F.A. Hihn did not have a finger in — he also owned extensive properties in San Francisco.

The Hihns entertained extensively in their imposing home which had more than 20 rooms. The gardens surrounding the house were the talk of the town. Rare shrubs, trees and flowers were brought there from many parts of the world. The gardens covered almost the entire block bounded by Chestnut, Church, Locust and Center Streets.

*continued on page 94*

*Stick style and Eastlake.*

4

*And the Hihn Mansion became the Santa Cruz City Hall.*

# The Grover Mansion

On Friday, January 1, 1869, Dwight W. Grover wrote in his diary: "A wet and rainy day. Father and I chopped some wood. We were all at home and its as lonesome as you please..."

Dwight Grover was about 16 years old when he wrote that, and the family was living near Soquel. The Grovers, three brothers, Frealon, Lyman and Whitney, came from Maine to California in 1850. They prospected for gold in the Mother Lode country, but by 1861 they had settled near Soquel on Bates Creek, to establish another kind of "gold mine" — a lumber mill.

The Grovers prospered and eventually there were four lumber mills in Santa Cruz County, two shingle mills, a finishing mill and drying yards where lumber was seasoned. There was also a flour mill in Santa Cruz on lower Pacific Avenue, and a mercantile business at the corner of Pacific and Soquel.

The Grover family donated lumber for the building of Soquel's Little White Church, according to Mrs. Hazel Grover Leonard, who makes her home in Santa Cruz.

For many years, she lived in one of three elegant homes built by Grovers on Walnut Avenue, next to Grover's Lane.

The house that is pictured was built by Hazel's grandfather, James Lyman Grover, in 1880. Dwight Grover had constructed a one-story Roman-Revival with Italianate details on the adjoining lot, in 1877. In 1887, Frealon Grover joined the other two by building a huge Eastlake style house on a third lot. The three Grover houses stood for years, side by side, but widely separated by formal gardens, carriage houses and ornate fences; they were *grandes dames* of another era. Monoliths. Monuments. Landmarks that struck awe in the haughtiest hearts.

In the photograph, from Mrs. Leonard's collection, one may see the wood sidewalk and fancy iron fence that fronted James Lyman Grover's mansion.

However, like many another relic of earlier eras, the two largest houses were torn down in the early 1930's to make way for "modern bungalows." Mrs. Leonard's home, the one-story house with its wealth of detailed wood trim, was demolished in 1967 to make way for apartments.

*Eastlake with tower.*

# Rennie House

The stately Rennie House stood at 514 Cliff Street on Beach Hill in Santa Cruz where William Rennie, its Scots builder and resident, could look out over the Pacific on which he had almost lost his life years before.

Bad fortune seemed to dog Rennie's footsteps wherever he traveled, beginning when he left his native Scotland in 1849 to seek his fortune as a carpenter in the New World, and ended up in the California gold fields.

Rennie started out originally for Canada, but by the time he got to Wisconsin, the weather was so cold that carpenter work was frozen to a standstill. California sounded interesting and he headed West.

"Nuggets as big as marbles to be had for the picking...Mountain stream beds paved with gold...Hillsides glittering with fortunes!" These early-day superlatives were rich mainly in adjectives and exaggeration. Nothing was said of aching backs and calloused hands, of cholera epidemics and freezing winter weather, of eggs at $1 each and claim jumpers with guns. Nor was any mention made of the perils of travel to the Golden Shores of California.

In the northern mines he found that the winter rains had set in, even in "sunny" California, so he traveled down to Sacramento with friends and found work on a brick building, the first to be built there, it is said.

When he heard news of a rich gold strike in Australia he joined 50 other eager gold-seekers, chartered a small British ship and set sail for down under. Arriving in Australia, Rennie made the unhappy discovery that he had followed another elusive will-o'-the-wisp that ended in a dust bowl.

Disappointed, heartsick and disillusioned, he got aboard a sailing ship to return to California. About 1,200 miles from Hawaii (the Sandwich Islands then), the ship foundered on a reef and went down. The men took to the lifeboats and drifted for days beneath the blazing tropic sun and beating rains.

They wandered the sea for two weeks without hope. Food was gone. The other boats disappeared. Desperately hungry, Rennie and his companions first ate the Captain's dog. Then they were able to catch a small shark and they ate that. They were on the thin edge of death when an American ship picked them up.

Rennie and his companions were taken to Hawaii where he waited two months for a ship going to California. But once back in that state, he settled down in the rich Sacramento Valley where he farmed and quickly prospered. In 1859 he — brave man — set sail for Scotland where he married Margaret Dawson.

In 1869 the prosperous couple came to Santa Cruz to live a more luxurious life. They first settled in a small cottage on the Cliff Street property where Rennie later built his mansion. The house was constructed in the early 1880's and stood until 1970 when it was razed.

From his Santa Cruz hilltop home William Rennie could look out in one direction over the Pacific which had once almost taken his life, and in the other over the fertile San Lorenzo River bed with its acres of fruit trees and promise of a future city.

*Eastlake with graceful touches.*

*continued on page 94*

# The Widow Wilson's 'Modern' Home

A "modern" home with both hot and cold running water was still something of a novelty in Santa Cruz in the 1880's.

The Widow Wilson had hers built in 1887 on the "high ground East of town." What was then outside the town, is very nearly in the center of it today, although the old house is gone.

The house stood alone for many years and from its veranda there was a fine view of Loma Prieta, the distinctive "dark hill" of early Spanish days.

Martha Wilson came to Santa Cruz as a widow, leaving a tragic story behind in Illinois. A native of Lancashire, England, Martha Pilkington Wilson numbered among her forebears Sir Richard Pilkington, first Bishop of Durham, remembered in history for his revision of the English Book of Common Prayer.

Martha came to New York as a child with her family, and later they moved to Illinois where her father died in 1830. A few years later, when she was visiting her older married sister in New York, Martha married Jasper Wilson, who had courted her in Illinois where their families were neighbors.

Jasper bought a large farm in Illinois and the Wilsons settled down to a prosperous and busy life, raising three children. Then, suddenly, in 1862, Jasper and two of their children died, probably victims of an epidemic. Mrs. Wilson then began to devote her life to the remaining son, David. They toured England in 1869, returning to the U.S. so David could enter the University of Illinois in 1870. But after a year at school his health failed.

Like a hen with one chick, Martha bundled up her frail son and brought him West for his health. They settled in Santa Cruz where Martha's brother, Thomas Pilkington, had a farm.

David regained his health and went to Washington State where he became a successful businessman. Martha led a busy social life in Santa Cruz, organizing the Women's Aid Society and serving as its first president. Her private charities were many and unsung, it is said. David Wilson and his bride, Emma Goodspeed Wilson, also lived in Martha's "modern house."

A year after she built her big home, Martha knew for sure she would spend the rest of her days in Santa Cruz. She went back to Illinois, had the bodies of her husband and two children disinterred and brought West, then reburied them in Santa Cruz IOOF Cemetery.

As long as she lived, Martha kept fresh flowers on their graves. Today she lies buried with them.

Her "modern" home was for years the piano studio of two talented sisters, Vera McKenna Clayton and Melba McKenna, who taught several generations of Santa Cruzans.

In 1968 the house was demolished to make way for a gasoline station.

Hulda McLean
1974

# Section II

# They Await Their Fate. . .

# Hotaling Building

## (McHugh-Bianchi)

### Pacific Garden Mall,
### Santa Cruz

*Hotaling Building stands on the site of the first general merchandise store to be located "down on the flat," in Santa Cruz. The first was a one-story frame building put up by Charles D. Eldon in 1851. Before that time, all commercial buildings were located on Mission Hill, around the Mission Santa Cruz Plaza. Eldon, who was the pioneer "downtown" grocer, sold out to the Cooper brothers in 1858 and his frame store was razed by A.P. Hotaling later. Hotaling Building is a fine example of the Victorian Italianate style of architecture, with quoins at its corners and a horizontal ornamented band with brackets near the roof line. A two-story structure, it was built completely of Santa Cruz County redwood. Windows are shelf-trimmed. Siding is shiplap.*

Progress...and paradox...a picture of what is happening today in Santa Cruz, historic Mission town on Monterey Bay.

The City of Santa Cruz is presently going through a period unlike anything in its past. This turbulent time has spawned factions, groups against or for almost any idea that is proposed. Some days one would suspect that the only issues unanimously approved today are motherhood, apple pie and the American Flag. And lately, the Flag and motherhood are taking their lumps. So that leaves apple pie.

One local question with which almost no one takes issue, is the restoration and preservation of Santa Cruz' old homes. People are buying them, repairing them, living in them and cherishing them. "Outsiders" who come to Santa Cruz exclaim with delight at the city's picturesque atmosphere, thanks to these senior structures.

It can be a different story with commercial buildings. Pacific Garden Mall, formerly Pacific Avenue, has a few left. One of the oldest, most meaningful to many people, is commonly referred to as the "McHugh and Bianchi Building," although it was built about 1886 by A.P. Hotaling, the man who built Santa Cruz' St. George Hotel in 1895. McHugh and Bianchi were the last to operate a grocery business in the building. For the past 25 years, activities went on as usual in the old structure, groceries were sold and delivered, meats and cheeses were dispensed. Then in 1971 the building changed hands, going to a savings and investment company. Plans for demolishing it and putting up a new structure were rumored, and the historic-minded citizens of the town got upset.

A number of minor skirmishes followed with charges from both sides. The historic-minded segment of the populace wanted the building saved. The new owners announced they were willing to investigate alternatives to tearing down the Hotaling Building, one of which would preserve its facade with a new structure behind it.

At the present time the whole affair is in limbo. The building has been listed in the National Register of Historic Places (October, 1972), along with Santa Cruz' Octagonal Hall of Records and two of the county's covered bridges. The Hotaling Building also has come to the attention of the California Heritage Council, which passed a resolution calling for its preservation (January, 1972).

Old and creaky as it may be today, the Hotaling Building has had an important part in the City's past, and it stands at the Lower Plaza, "crossroads" of the community in early days. It is one of the first downtown buildings, and the first on the Pacific Garden Mall, that people see as they enter the main section of Santa Cruz.

Before 1946, the store was Lease and Wettstein Grocers. And before that it was C.D. Hinkle's Cash Store. Hinkle, an Indiana boy who came to Santa Cruz and made good, opened his store in 1894. His stock also included such non-edibles as bicycles, dry goods and plows. Business was good for Mr. Hinkle. He operated two horse and wagon deliveries each day and employed Etta Snedecor, James D. Tait, Arthur Owens and Marion Woodruff to wait on customers. Grocers in those days also handled things like kerosene for the household lamps, the lamps themselves, canning jars and such, as well as exotic foods like dates from Araby and watermelons in season.

*continued on page 94*

# School Street Adobe

### 136 School Street, Santa Cruz

The old adobe is as skittish as an old maid; she won't tell her age and there's no way to pry it out of her. Even with her roof off and her ribs exposed, there's no way to tell. Her exact number of years remains a mystery.

A plaque says the adobe was built in 1810; other educated guesses place it earlier, about 1796. The mission was built in 1793-94 and it is known that each mission of the California chain had its guardhouse for soldiers; in fact the soldiers' quarters were usually built right along with the Mission sanctuary. Protection was a necessity.

Here again, history is mute. The original purpose of the School Street Adobe remains as much a mystery as its age. It is known that detached adobe buildings in its area housed a school, Indian women's sleeping quarters and a guardhouse. This one remaining adobe of those early days is believed by many to have been the guardhouse.

When Santa Cruz Mission was secularized and turned over to civil authorities in 1834-35, some of the church property was divided among the few remaining Costanoan Indians. The School Street Adobe and a few surrounding acres were the property of Indians. In 1838 Jose de la Rodriguez paid them two cows and two mules for a portion of their property. The other half of the adobe was sold to Patrick Neary in 1865. The unique building was Santa Cruz' first duplex. The two portions were separated by a five-foot thick adobe wall.

The Rodriguez and Neary families retained their portions and made their homes in them until 1957 when the State of California purchased the historic building. Leading the campaign to have the adobe designated and preserved as a State Historical Landmark were members of Santa Cruz Historical Society. Miss Alice Neary sold her half outright; Miss Cornelia Hopcroft, a Rodriguez heir, retained a life tenancy and still makes her home in her half of the adobe. The Neary half houses an antique shop.

In 1965 when rains threatened to melt a portion of the adobe, the State Division of Beaches and Parks reroofed the building. When the old roof was removed, evidence was uncovered that indicates it was originally a one-story adobe instead of two. And so the mysteries accumulate.

Upstairs in 1854, Santa Cruz Masonic Lodge was organized and came into being.

Today there is a rumor that the City of Santa Cruz might consider taking over the building in the near future. A great asset to the entire idea of museum and meeting place, is the garden on the hill behind the adobe; it looks out over the entire city, with a huge redwood tree framing the view.

In the interim, the most historic building in the City of Santa Cruz sits on Mission Hill, a relic of yesterday, waiting for tomorrow to happen.

*Built circa 1810 but some authorities place it as early as 1796. No record of actual date. It is the only remaining original adobe of the Santa Cruz Mission compound.*

# Hagemann House

## (Live Oak Ranch)

### 105 Mentel Avenue, Santa Cruz

*This structure is often referred to as a "cottage," but what it might lack in size, it more than makes up in elaborate wood and metal trim, and towers — two of them! The house has been labeled Italianate Victorian, but the towers give it an Oriental, almost Persian or Moorish feeling, which the lacy woodwork enhances. Inside, the house is little changed. The original wallpapers are intact in the main rooms and the entry hall. The Gunns, present owners, have furnished the house with their own collection of beautiful antiques as well as Mrs. Gunn's sculpture and the fine metal sculpture of her partner, John Sillstrop. Even the shirred white silk curtains at the living room windows are replicas of those that hung there when the Hagemanns were in residence, as seen in a photograph of the time, now in the Gunns' possession. In addition to two "parlors," master bedroom, dining room and kitchen downstairs, the house has four bedrooms upstairs..."And no bathrooms!" Mr. Gunn jokes.*

Situated at 105 Mentel Avenue on one of the largest single-dwelling properties remaining in the City of Santa Cruz, this unusual house with its twin towers cannot be viewed from the street.

It is approached by way of a long, winding driveway through a grove of Eucalyptus and Cypress trees. The property includes about seven and one-third acres, with wild azalea thickets and ferns in a ravine, coveys of quail, raccoons and oppossums, a lively population of the small creatures who can manage to survive with city life surrounding them. To the south, a short walk away over meadow and grassy pastureland, is Santa Cruz Small Crafts Harbor.

The present owners are Mr. and Mrs. Charles H. Gunn. Mrs. Gunn is a sculptress of note. They purchased the house and acreage from the Fergusons, the Fergusons from the Israelsons, the Israelsons from the Kinzli family. Before that, the property was owned by Frederick Hagemann, an associate of Claus Spreckels. The towered house, very ornate in its decorations, was built by Hagemann before 1880 and started life as a farm house of much simpler design. Sometime in the 1880's the towers and front rooms were added by Hagemann, as well as the gingerbread that gives the house an unusual appeal. He also built a beautiful fence which survives.

Frederick Hagemann's Live Oak Ranch originally had 110 acres; windmills furnished the water power and huge old oak trees gave the place its name. He raised wheat, cattle, horses, hogs and chickens. He also dabbled in other ventures, and built the Hagemann Hotel on Pacific Avenue.

Hagemann was born in Hanover, Germany, in 1824, came to New York in 1852, then visited South America and was shipwrecked at Cape Horn. He arrived in San Francisco in 1853, penniless, worked in the gold mines, lost his money, opened a shoe store in San Francisco and — finally — had a bit of luck. In 1861 he was prosperous enough to sail to Germany and spend four years. However, he returned to the U.S. in 1866 and bought Claus Spreckels' interest in the Albany Brewery.

In 1878 Hagemann retired from the brewery and came to Santa Cruz to live the life of gentleman farmer. In those days his Live Oak Ranch was considered "way out in the country." His first wife died in 1876 and in 1877 he married Amelia Cassuben, a native of Holstein. It was for her that he built his farm house.

Today the 110 acres have shrunk to less than eight, and the City limits have crept out to enfold the property with its "blue gum forest" and hidden ravine.

Currently there is discussion of extending Broadway-Brommer Street through its acres to the south, demolishing the barn which is Mrs. Gunn's studio, and barely skirting the house itself.

"If the City would be interested in creating a park, and would build a bridge to span the ravine where the wild azalea grows, we may consider giving part of our property for use as the park," states Charles Gunn, present owner. He makes it clear that the gift would depend on several conditions that would have to be met by the City. He and Mrs. Gunn are concerned about the ecological impact of earth fill (instead of a bridge) to span the ravine, for one thing.

He points out that hiking and bicycle paths could extend from Live Oak Ranch through the undulating countryside to the Small Crafts

*continued on page 95*

18

## Leslie Brick Building

Most passersby would not look twice — or maybe even once, at this building. If they did look, their thought might be: It's a poor imitation of a Mission Revival style.

Not so — not really. Underneath its many coats of plaster and paint, there exists the first brick building to be constructed in Santa Cruz. This fact is barely known today.

Nothing is known of the man named Leslie who built the structure at the top of Mission Hill. Even the year of construction is a mystery, but in the late Ernest Otto's writings there are several mentions of this building as "the first brick building in Santa Cruz."

A fair guess would be 1850, because by 1852 the center of "business" was moving down onto "the flat" where it is centered today.

Leslie, whoever he was, apparently did not remain long in Santa Cruz. The brick building was constructed with living quarters upstairs, a common plan in that era. Originally it had plain rectangular windows with dark iron shutters. It is built of the soft red brick that was manufactured in one of several brick yards in Santa Cruz. When Mission Hill School was located next door, the building served as neighborhood grocery (and penny candy shop) with living quarters still upstairs. That was in the 1920's and 1930's. Interesting to note, this is probably the most historic brick structure in Santa Cruz, antedating the famed Flatiron brick building down in the flat.

20

# Section III

# Success Stories, Old and New

# 'An Ornament to the Corner'

### 201 Maple Street, Santa Cruz

*Built about 1869-70 [the exact date is unknown], this fine example of the Stick Style shows how attractive that decoration can be when properly painted and landscaped. The house serves as a subtle reminder that these "stick" and "carpenter Gothic" houses were originally intended to blend into foliage which softened their effect, and they were often painted tan or green. Their wood trim, "board nailed on top of board," often copied Gothic stone traceries. Roy Rydell, present owner and restorer of the house, has carried out the "stick" feeling in the picket fence he designed to surround it.*

In the last two years a startling transformation has taken place at 201 Maple Street — corner of Maple and Cedar Streets, Santa Cruz.

A rather nondescript old stick style house has evolved from ugly duckling into near-swan. Responsible for the change is Roy Rydell, Santa Cruz landscape architect who designed the Pacific Garden Mall landscaping for the city. He also has co-authored a new book on landscape gardening by *Sunset*.

What ever possessed Mr. Rydell to take on such an undistinguished house in a rather run-down area of town?

"The challenge it presented," he explains. "It's quite a challenge to do something with a substandard house, to bring out and develop its possibilities."

The house at 201 Maple hasn't had many possibilities for becoming an eye-catcher, since it evolved out of a plain farmhouse built there about 1869-70. The house is located on what was once the Rodriguez Tract, became the property of Frederick A. Hihn and was sold to a Mrs. McAlmond. In 1869 she sold it back to Mr. Hihn and it isn't clear whether or not the house was standing there at that time.

However, when Hihn sold it again, to Joseph B. Hickman, in 1873, the house probably was there. It passed from Hickman to Victory DeCarly in 1878, and then to F. E. J. Canney the same year. By 1881 it was in the hands of Mrs. Trefry who sold it to Charles M. Collins of the Collins and Maxwell Grocery firm.

Collins doubled the size of the original house and hired an architect to bestow upon it what style it has ever possessed. Daniel A. Damkroger, the architect who designed Weeks House and several other notable structures in Santa Cruz, was to completely remodel and enlarge the house at 201 Maple.

Work started in October of 1887 and by December was almost complete. The house had 10 rooms and face-lift: cost, $2,000. Actually, the cost was whittled down to $1,800, according to an article in the *Santa Cruz Surf* which also proclaimed that the remodeled house "...Is an ornament to the corner..." In those days it was the corner of Maple Street and Grand Avenue. Apparently Grand Avenue became Cedar Street sometime between then and now.

The house must have enjoyed a few years of solid respectability, but when Roy Rydell acquired it in September, 1972, it was difficult to see possibilities. It had been used as a rooming house for many years — a sad fate that falls to the lot of many of these big old houses. Rooms had been cut up, makeshift cooking areas had to be removed and everything had to be rewired.

Today the "ornament" is that again — thanks to landscape gardening and a coat of dark paint on the house. An attractive picket fence has been built. "We found traces of the old one when we were working in the garden," he explains.

There are two apartments upstairs and Mr. Rydell's landscape gardening office downstairs.

Passers-by again notice the house and admire it for what it is — an "ornament to the corner."

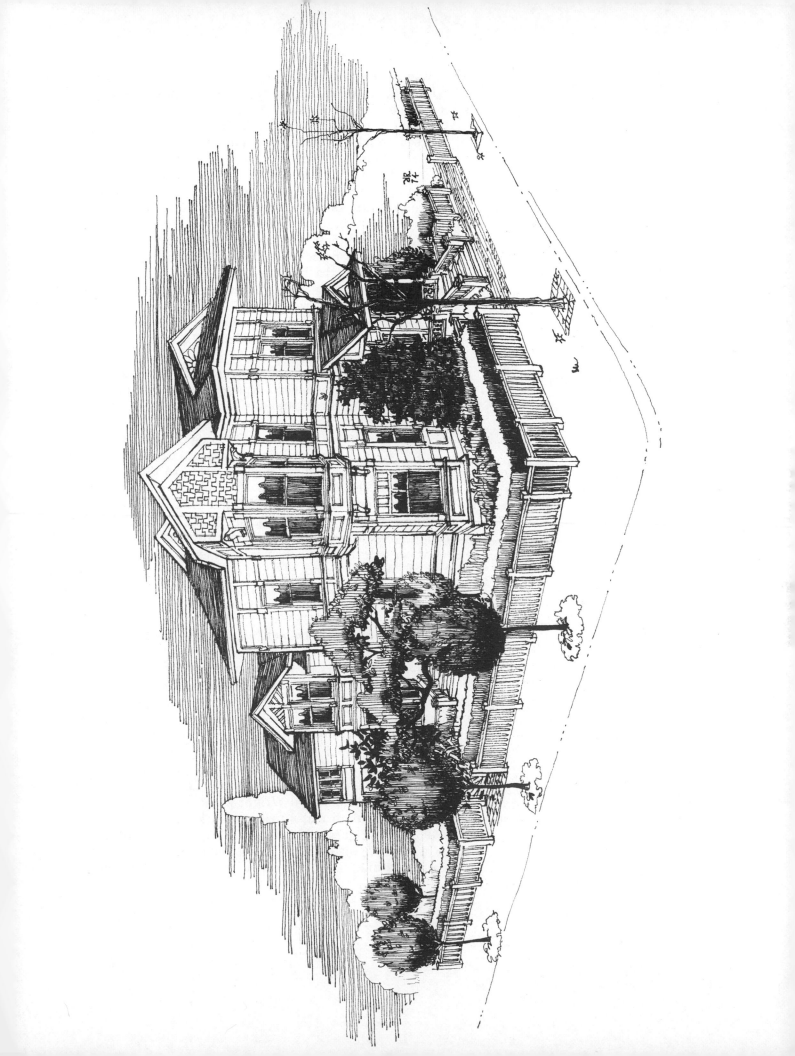

# The Countess' Log Cabin

## (Babbling Brook)

1025 Laurel Street,
Santa Cruz

*This is a true log cabin, built with whole redwood logs, the bark left on. Built in 1909-1910, the house was later embellished with decorative iron work over windows and inside, made by Otar the Lampmaker of Santa Cruz, who had his studio on Pacific Avenue. The log house is reminiscent of the Swiss chalet style, with a balcony from the second story portion. Upper area of the second story is redwood shingles. The log cabin is located at 1025 Laurel Street, on a hillside where the historic Majors Creek gushes forth to meander past its foundations.*

On Laurel Street in Santa Cruz, just midway on the hill, there sits an old log cabin — real logs, no fake about it. And as California wood structures go, it can decently be called "old."

A stream of water comes shooting out of the hill at its feet. The little creek wanders through the garden below the log cabin and disappears again, to lose itself in Neary Lagoon.

The log house is named Babbling Brook and it has had quite a career since it was built some 64 years ago by Mr. and Mrs. Charlie Place, touring actors who decided they wanted to settle down in Santa Cruz. However, after a short time, the lure of the footlights got to them again, and they sold their log house and left to go on tour. Mrs. Place's stage name was Mabel Thompson.

The Places chose the hillside location in the first place because across the street in those days there stood the remnants of an historic and picturesque water wheel — a leftover from Kirby's Tannery. The tannery extended along the top of the hill and its water wheel made use of the little creek which still comes gushing out of the hill below the log house.

Like many other natural landmarks in Santa Cruz County, the course of the creek has been changed in recent years with the widening of Laurel Street and the building of underground waterways.

For years the place was known as the Log Cabin. It passed to Mr. and Mrs. Peter Rovnianek who came to Santa Cruz from Chicago. He was for several years Consul from Slovakia to the United States. The Rovnianeks enlarged the log cabin a bit and developed gardens.

The next owners of note were Mr. and Mrs. Charles Chandler. He was a San Francisco attorney and she was a countess — by wishful thinking, some still say. A native of Austria, she is said to have received her title through a former marriage to the late Count Nikolai of Austria. Whether or not she had a right to the title, she claimed it and was always — but *always* — addressed as Madame Countess. Madame Countess Florenz de Chandler was the complete title she used.

The Chandlers were extremely social and entertained lavishly and often, in their log house. The Countess was a very large woman much given to gallons of jewels as well as her title. She was the person responsible for developing the terraces in the gardens and for installing the fine ironwork on doors, windows and fireplaces. The ornamental ironwork was created by Otar the Lampmaker who had a studio on Pacific Avenue but whose fame went much further afield.

The Chandlers sold their log cabin and took an apartment on Beach Hill in the Palais Monte Carlo, then left Santa Cruz to live in Florida where she died as the result of a fall in 1951. The log house went to Mr. and Mrs. Lloyd Wright who operated a restaurant in it, then leased it out to other restaurateurs.

In 1962 the Wrights sold and the log house changed hands several times before 1973 when Frances McReynolds Smith got it. "Got it" is the correct term..."I had to have it," she says with a smile. The new

*continued on page 95*

24

# Smith House

### 250 Ocean View Avenue, Santa Cruz

*Queen Anne with Eastlake touches. Corner of Ocean View Avenue and Windham Street, built circa 1890.*

Indian fighter — and lawyer. That was Lucas F. Smith who came to Santa Cruz in 1888. While he found adventure in fighting Indians and sending a murderer to the gallows, his Southern-born wife, the former Della Gouldy, preferred to give tea parties.

Southern hospitality was a memorable feature of the Smith home. And even Lucas, who became presiding judge of Santa Cruz Superior Court, learned to trip the light fantastic at Della's parties.

The Smith home was built by Lucas to house their six children as well as to serve as a social headquarters. It was constructed several years after he brought his family to Santa Cruz. It contained a full attic, three bedrooms and a sitting room upstairs, two parlors, dining room and kitchen downstairs.

The house passed out of the Smith family a number of years ago, and today it is one of the showplaces of the town--thanks to a couple who bought it, restored it and made it their home for about 10 years.

Mr. and Mrs. Ed Perkins performed a labor of love on the old house, retaining the natural redwood woodwork and features such as the pressed metal paneling. The major change was in the kitchen, which was completely modernized although not structurally changed in any way — it's still a huge, old-fashioned looking kitchen. The Perkins' also added a powder room and several bathrooms. And in 1972 they sold to Mr. and Mrs. Edward C. Sumpf who now live in the house that Lucas Smith built.

Peaceful Santa Cruz of the 1880's must have seemed a quiet backwater to Lucas Smith. A native of Indiana, he fought in Regiment G of the Indiana Volunteers at Chickamauga and under General Sherman during the famed "march to the sea." After the Civil War he did not go back to the family farm, but entered University of Michigan where he graduated in 1868. He then went to Texas where he became district attorney of Bonham, and served as prosecutor in one of the 1870's most notorious criminal cases: the State of Texas vs. Stephen M. Ballew.

Ballew had murdered James P. Golden of Illinois, then had wed Golden's sister while wearing her murdered brother's clothing.

Lucas Smith pursued Ballew through the courts and finally brought him to justice at the end of a rope. For this, Smith gained the gratitude of everyone — except Ballew, of course — and even received a complimentary resolution from the State of Illinois.

From Texas, Smith moved to positions and law partnerships in New Mexico, where he also organized a band of Indian fighters, to Missouri, then back to Texas. There he married Della in 1882.

In Santa Cruz six years later, he seemed satisfied to settle down to a steady law career, raising a family of two sons and four daughters, and making an appearance at Della's social affairs. The 10-room house offered the perfect setting, although in recent years, one of the Smith daughters was heard to remark: "That kitchen was a killer!"

The sons, both of whom entered law, are dead now. Three of the four daughters live in Santa Cruz yet.

Hulda McLean
1974

# The Weeks House

## 724 California Street, Santa Cruz

*This magnificent structure with its cupolas, tower, gables, scrolls, flutings, knobs and swirls, was built about 1886 for Thomas Jefferson Weeks. One of Santa Cruz' truly important Eastlake houses with touches of Queen Anne, it cost $9,000 — a princely sum for a home in those days. One report has it that LeBaron R. Oliver was the architect; another states that Daniel Damkroger designed the elaborate home. Complete with brackets, a finial on its tower and quatrefoil trim on porches, Weeks House is something to see, indeed. Arched windows are finished with decorated trim. Siding is redwood shiplap. Porch pillars are elaborately turned and embellished. The house originally stood on Walnut Avenue hill, commanding a magnificent panorama of Monterey Bay and the Santa Cruz Beach where Weeks lived in a shack years before. It was moved to its present location in 1913 to make way for Santa Cruz High School. The interior is as fascinating as the ornate exterior, with a hallway paneled with pressed leather and one fireplace inlaid with redwood burl.*

Thomas Jefferson Weeks built a house that was acclaimed at the time as "One of the most commodious and attractive in the entire county..."

Today the Weeks House is one of a handful of Santa Cruz' truly spectacular Victorians. One account (Guinn 1903 *History and Biographies of the State of California*) notes that Thomas Weeks built his magnificent home in 1890.

In any event, the house must have seemed like a castle to Thomas, who, poor as a church mouse when he arrived in California, lived in a shack on Santa Cruz beach at first.

A native of Wayne, Kennebec County, Maine, he came to Santa Cruz in 1849 after trying his hand at the mines. In the Mother Lode he found that just plain existing was extremely costly, and besides, he didn't like the work of mining. He was a stone cutter by trade and used to working hard. But he found mining "uncongenial."

When he and a friend arrived in Santa Cruz in November, 1849, they bought the cabin off an old schooner and set it up on the beach as their "home." Looking around for a way to make a living, Weeks decided to try his hand at raising potatoes — probably with memories still vivid of the cost of potatoes in the mining areas. He and a partner named DeLong rented a few acres from Judge William Blackburn, planted potatoes and raised 400 sacks to the acre, the first year. He had rented 25 acres at $15 per acre; his crop made him $5,000. The following year, Judge Blackburn raised the rent to $100 per acre, but potato prices were so good that Weeks and DeLong each made another $5,000. Profits decreased thereafter in potatoes, as everyone planted them and the market was glutted. But Weeks was resourceful; he went into the teaming business — hauling redwood lumber was big business a few years later, and he planted an orchard, 25 acres of fruit. He also invested in land and eventually owned 86 fine acres. His property extended from Walnut Avenue to Laurel Street, and Mission Street to Chestnut Avenue.

In 1854 Thomas Weeks married Margaret M. Morgan, a niece of Judge Blackburn, and they had three children, two of whom lived to adulthood. In later years Thomas was active as a realtor and was known as a raiser of fine horses.

Thomas and Margaret built their home on the hill above the Walnut Avenue and Lincoln Street junction, although today it is located on California Street, about a block away. The huge old house was moved to make way for Santa Cruz High School and the Weeks orchard and gardens became the high school football field and site of its gymnasium.

The house has passed through many hands, down over the years. Today it is the home of Mr. and Mrs. Robert Page, who treasure every detail.

Hulda McLean
1974

# "The Breakers" Looks Out Over the Breakers

707 Pelton Avenue,
Santa Cruz

*The Breakers rises in majestic simplicity on the corner of Pelton and West Cliff Drive, little changed from the day it was completed in 1876. Its windows were large and many, with a breath-taking sweep to the east of Monterey Bay, Santa Cruz City, the Municipal Wharf and waterfront. The house is built of redwood, as are most of Santa Cruz' fine old homes. Its trim is simple, spool and spindle in the eaves above the windows, and many small spindles around the top of the porches. Siding is shiplap. Style is Eastlake, done with great restraint.*

"The Breakers" stands at the corner of Pelton and West Cliff Drive in Santa Cruz, almost exactly as it looked when it was built in 1876 by a Methodist bishop and his wife.

The spacious gardens were laid out in a day when taxes were low and upkeep was a small item. The carriage house usually sheltered several servants as well as the family's wheeled vehicles. A gardener's cottage was a practical investment. All these are remnants of an elegant, bygone era.

The fine old house at the corner of West Cliff Drive and Pelton Avenue echoes two names prominent in California and Colorado annals: Warren and Iliff.

Bishop and Mrs. Henry Warren visited Santa Cruz for several summers before they bought the West Cliff property and built their gracious home. It was first called "Epworth by the Sea" for the English birthplace of John Wesley, founder of Methodism. Later the name was changed to "The Breakers," more in keeping with its enchanting view of Monterey Bay.

The Warrens came to Santa Cruz from Colorado where Mrs. Warren owned extensive ranch holdings and was known as the "Cattle Queen." She formerly had been married to a member of the wealthy Iliff family of Denver, and her gifts established the Iliff School of Theology there.

In "The Breakers," Bishop Warren had his own book-lined study where he wrote many of the stirring sermons for which he was known throughout the Methodist-Episcopal Church. While he studied and wrote, his children climbed down a set of steps which clung to the cliff and led to the beach and bay below. The entire family could be seen almost daily, enjoying a dip in the surf.

Mrs. Warren spent much time planning the gardens. Lawns and flowers were planted and rows of stately elm trees bordered the streets. A rare Century Tree still thrives in the garden facing West Cliff Drive.

When the Warren family drove to church or downtown to shop, they rode in style. They owned sleek, spirited horses; their harness was polished to a high gloss, their carriages were the finest money could buy.

Eventually Bishop and Mrs. Warren bought an entire block facing the Bay. It was bounded by West Cliff Drive, Santa Cruz Avenue, Gharkey Street and Lighthouse Avenue. When erosion ate away part of the cliff, the property line was moved back. In the 1880's a portion of the Warren property was deeded to a son, William Iliff, who built himself a home of solid concrete — a novelty in those days. For years, members of the Warren and Iliff families spent vacations at "The Breakers."

Last member of the family to live there was a daughter, Edna Iliff Briggs. She died in San Francisco in 1951 and as part of her estate, "The Breakers" was sold. Today it is an apartment house, very appropriately named "The Breakers Apartments."

# Cliff-Crest

### 407 Cliff Street, Santa Cruz

*A Victorian, unusually open in design, architect unknown. Built about 1870, and the solarium and belvedere were added in 1903-04.*

William and Jennie Jeter purchased Cliff-Crest in the 1890's. Those were busy years for Bill Jeter — he was Lieutenant-Governor of the State of California, serving from 1895 to 1899. He was also a practicing lawyer, had served as chairman of Santa Cruz Democratic Committee in 1882, was a member of Santa Cruz City Council during the "boys' administration," and was a banker as well as lawyer and politician.

The single accomplishment for which Mr. Jeter is best remembered today is the magnificent stand of redwoods (*Sequoia sempervirens*) near Felton. The Jeters were early-day ecologists before that word had been coined. He organized the Big Trees Company from his death bed in a Santa Cruz hospital, in order to save the redwoods that are today called Henry Cowell Redwoods State Park.

William Jeter came to Santa Cruz in 1877 from Missouri after first visiting San Francisco. In 1885 he married Jennie Bliss who was the daughter of Moses B. Bliss, and the couple settled in a home on Walnut Avenue. He had completed his law education in San Francisco.

William became District Attorney of Santa Cruz County in 1884 and served three terms, or six years. During the "boys' administration," which was noted for constructing a sewer system and obtaining public ownership of the city water system, he headed the ordinance and finance committees. Sidewalk and street paving was accomplished with Santa Cruz County's own bitumen, also during that administration.

One old account states: "...giving the City of Santa Cruz the enviable reputation of having more first-class sidewalks than any city in the world of like population..." and "...all of which has contributed to placing Santa Cruz in the front row of wide-awake, enterprising cities..."

In 1893 William Jeter became president of County Bank of Santa Cruz and remained so until 1930 — something of a record.

He and Jennie entertained a great deal in the home they later bought on Cliff Street, Beach Hill. It stands about 1,000 feet from the Bay, on approximately one-half acre complete with large carriage house.

The home includes a drawing room, living room, dining room, solarium, kitchen, three bedrooms, baths and belvedere. Fireplaces in the dining and living rooms work. The solarium contains stained glass that is truly unusual, echoing the colors and feeling of Gauguin paintings. In the dining room there are leaded glass china cabinet doors. The entire house is constructed of redwood with a total square footage of about 3,300 feet. One special addition by the Jeters was a curved handrail on the staircase.

However, the garden was lavished with as much attention as the house. The Jeters were friends of John McLaren, the landscape designer of Golden Gate Park in San Francisco. A number of unusual plantings, still thriving after more than 50 years, include Belgian Laurel, Japanese Camellia, a giant mattress vine, several unusual fuschias, two fine Gingko trees, a deep purple tulip tree and two palm trees.

*continued on page 95*

32

# The Cookhouse

University of California at
Santa Cruz Campus

The Cowell Ranch Cookhouse always was red, although all the other ranch buildings were whitewashed.

It was in use as a cookhouse from about the 1880's into the early 1950's, as part of the Henry Cowell Ranch operation. John Dong, the Cowell's last cook, presided over the cookhouse during the lifetime of Samuel (Harry) Cowell who died on February 1, 1955, at the age of 93.

Harry Cowell breathed his last in his San Francisco home, 70 miles from the rolling ranch hills of his Santa Cruz acreage, but he loved horses and he enjoyed nothing so much as a ride over the Ranch's broad meadows and through its thick redwood forests.

The Cookhouse was where ranch hands ate, and sometimes Harry ate there too when he was in Santa Cruz. Equipment in the place consisted of an old wood-burning stove, a sink, a few tables and chairs, and coal oil lamps. The building had no electricity until after 1949. A small screened cabin at one end was the meat cooler, and a pigsty out front was the garbage disposal.

The Cookhouse actually stands on the site of the earliest quarry on the Cowell property, which first was mined for limestone by Isaac Davis and Albion P. Jordan. In 1865 Henry Cowell, native of Massachusetts, bought out Jordan's limestone interests, and in 1888 he acquired Davis' portion and owned it all. There were approximately 2,000 acres of pasture dotted with huge old oak trees, and redwood forests.

The Ranch Cookhouse's future was assured when, on March 17, 1961, the Regents of the University of California announced their decision to found a new branch of the University on the Cowell Ranch at Santa Cruz.

In December of that year the Cowell Foundation deeded the property to the Regents.

In 1964 the Cookhouse became the "stove office," after renovation by the University's Planning and Construction unit. In January, 1965, Chancellor Dean E. McHenry moved in and the main conversation piece in his office was the old wood cook stove which has been there ever since. The lower floor in the Cookhouse served as offices for Page Smith, first Provost of Cowell College which was the first college to be established at the new University of California at Santa Cruz.

When Chancellor McHenry moved into Central Services, a new building, the Cookhouse served as office for a parade of University officials, and finally, for the University Security and Parking Departments.

Built into the hillside, the building's foundation is stone and concrete; the structure itself is redwood lumber. It is still painted the traditional barn red — and the old iron cook stove is still intact in what is now the upstairs office.

In recent years, Elizabeth Spedding Calciano, who heads the University's Regional Oral History project, got a group of old-timer Cowell employes together to talk about the Cowell Ranch. Harold Richey, George Cardiff, Claud and his brother Frank Lazarotti were reminiscing, and the Lazarotti boys recalled that their father had built part of the stone foundation. Cardiff said he recalled seeing the cookhouse there in 1890 when he was hiking through the Ranch.

34

*Upper photo: The old cook house of the Cowell Ranch, now being used for offices of the University of California, Santa Cruz.*
*Above: The old stove is still being used — as a bookshelf in the office.*
*On right: Interior of present offices.*

# The Willey
# Home Has Gone
# the 'Full Circle'

105 Sylvar Street,
Santa Cruz

*Redwood paneling, mellowed with the years and polished to the fine patina of old rosewood — Henry Willey used redwood from Santa Cruz County forests for his house. Only the main room floors are hardwood.*

*Built in 1893, Willey House is late Eastlake with several fine stained glass windows. Notable are the porch railings, the brackets and ornamental box beneath the window over the main entry. Brackets also adorn the underside of the second story porch which is supported on slender columns. The house is finished in smooth siding with one wide band of ornamental shingles under the eaves.*

The Henry Willey house started life as a home, went through stages of becoming a factory and a convent, and now, once again, is a home.

The Willey house sits at the corner of Mission Street and Sylvar, on the original site of its neighboring house, the Alzina home. The little frame Alzina house was moved over to make way for its more elegant, but historically not so important, neighbor. The Alzina structure is the city's oldest frame house.

When Henry Willey came to Santa Cruz in the late 1800's, the property at the corner of Mission and Sylvar was surrounded with a high board fence. Henry was the nephew of the Rev. Samuel Hopkins Willey, one of the founders of University of California. The Rev. Hopkins, after seeing his dream of a great University come true in Berkeley in 1868, came down to Santa Cruz to serve as pastor of the First Congregational Church.

Henry arrived at the home of his esteemed uncle in 1876. He had been destined (by his father) for the ministry, but finances had made that impossible. Instead, in Santa Cruz, Henry established a store: "Henry Willey Co. Hardware and Crockery, 72-74 Pacific Avenue."

Henry prospered so well that he became the first president of the People's Savings Bank. And he met a dark-eyed young widow in the mid-'80's, Mary Weldon Sinnott — always called "Mrs. Molly" after they married. Mary and her sister, Sara Weldon Gamble, had operated the old Quincy Hall Seminary for girls in Santa Cruz. The school moved to San Francisco as the Van Ness Seminary, then became the well-known Miss Hamlin's School for Girls.

Henry and his bride lived happily in the large house he built for her at the corner of Mission and Sylvar, for four years. Then Mrs. Molly and their infant son died in childbirth. For seven years Henry was a lonely widower — and then he met a blue-eyed music teacher, Frances Lockhart. In 1898 "Miss Fanny" became Mrs. Henry Willey and brought new life into the big house on the hill. The Willeys lived there until 1926 when they sold the house and moved to Monterey.

Mrs. George W. Cooper, the next owner, rented the house to Mrs. Helen Mowry who operated a lampshade factory there for a few years. The socially prominent Harry Hastings family of San Mateo also lived in the house briefly. In 1943 Mrs. Cooper sold the house to the Daughters (Sisters) of Charity, with the sale price between $2,000 and $3,000 — almost unbelievable. The nuns lived in it for just a few months, until the Dominican Sisters arrived to take their place as local parochial school teachers. The twelve Dominican nuns lived there and taught until 1954 when the Catholic Church sold the house to Robert Dodt, who sold to Mrs. Gwendolyn Niemeyer, who sold to Mitch Keil in 1973.

The house was built of redwood, which was also used for ornate paneling in the living and dining rooms, and for the big sliding doors which separate them. The floors are parquet hardwood. A small conservatory opened off the south porch and the dining room, and in Mrs. Molly's day it was always filled with begonias and ferns, and a large cage of canary birds. Out in the front garden a great magnolia tree, a date palm and a monkey tree flourished.

*continued on page 95*

36

# Alzina House

109 Sylvar Street,
Santa Cruz

From shipboard to sheriff — the life of Santa Cruz County's first "lawman" was never dull. And when he left the sea, he settled down in a little frame house on Holy Cross Plaza, across from Mission Santa Cruz.

Francisco Alzina ran away from his native Minorca in 1821, stowing away aboard a U.S. ship bound for America. The ship happened to be *Old Ironsides*, or the *USS Constitution*, which he boarded while at anchor in Barcelona Harbor. When safely at sea, Alzina made himself known. He was running away from military conscription. When the ship docked at Norfolk, Virginia, Alzina found a good position with Commodore Chauncey who was president of the U.S. Naval Hospital there.

In a few years, perhaps homesick to see his parents, Alzina sailed back to Spain. After a visit, he boarded the *USS Delaware* for the return trip to the United States — a trip which turned into a wild adventure. The *Delaware* was bringing the huge, heavy statue of Christopher Columbus to Washington, D.C. During the trip a storm came up, the five pieces of the work of art shifted dangerously in the ship's hold, and almost sank the ship.

Alzina went to sea again for the third and last time, when rumors of war with Mexico took him to Mazatlan. This trip took him around the ill-famed Horn, notorious for its deadly currents and chronic bad weather. When Alzina arrived in Monterey, Alta California, in 1846, he must have decided he had had enough of the sea. He came over to Santa Cruz and settled down to become a clerk in the court of Alcalde William Blackburn.

In 1848 Francisco Alzina married Maria Gonzales. And it has always been said that the lumber for the home they built at 109 Sylvar Street, was hauled down the coast from Maria's father's Rancho Pescadero.

Francisco and Maria lived out their lives in the little house, raising 14 children. Francisco became the first Sheriff of the newly-created Santa Cruz County in 1850, and served for eight years. He died in 1887.

Maria outlived her husband by a good number of years; their son Enoch, who became a deputy sheriff of Santa Cruz County, made his home with her in the family home.

Maria, as long as she lived, could be seen every morning of her life, dressed in dark skirts, black shawl over her head, crossing the Plaza to go to mass in Holy Cross Church.

Today the house still sits at 109 Sylvar Street, looking out on a scene that has changed from the days of the Costanoan Indians and Franciscan priests, to busy auto traffic.

New owners, Mr. and Mrs. Jason Goldstein, are intrigued with the house's long history and plan to retain its delightful character.

*The oldest wood frame house in Santa Cruz, built circa 1850. Fireplace added in more recent years. Early adobe Hispanic style.*

# Halsey House

## 207 Mission Street, Santa Cruz

*Probably the finest example of Eastlake style still standing in Santa Cruz, Halsey House was built about 1890. It stands at 270 Mission Street and still has its original carriage house in back. Fireplaces are French Towle work, handpainted with turkey feathers to simulate marble. Locks, hinges and knobs downstairs are all the original brass. Doors have "woodgraining," a Victorian fad wherein paint and varnish were mixed and applied to paneling to simulate wood graining. The wallpaper border in the front parlor, painted ceilings in the parlor and dining room are originals. Floors are redwood, with fir or pine in the kitchen. Careful restoration work was carried on by Mrs. Franklin Mieuli, owner, before the house passed to Mr. and Mrs. Willard W. Morris in 1972. The ceiling panels containing the popular Victorian stork motif were restored by John Faulkner for Mrs. Mieuli. The upstairs bath was left alone with its tub on legs, while the kitchen and downstairs bath were modernized.*

For years the house has stood, tall and commanding. Its imposing facade seems to demand that all eyes turn to it as they pass by on Mission Street.

Above the front door the white boards loom up, up and up, to a third story tower with windows all around it. As a child, walking by to school on Mission Hill, I used to speculate about that tower — dreaming of it as an enchanted place in which to sit and read, or just look out over the town and Monterey Bay. And today I still wonder if anyone ever went up into that magic crow's nest on top of the huge old house.

My third grade teacher lived there. Miss Alice Halsey was her name, and she and her sister Clara — both teachers — made their home in the house with the tower. How I envied them. They walked to the schools where they taught, Miss Alice to Mission Hill and Mrs. Clara (Taylor) to Bay View or Laurel.

The Halsey sisters were leftovers from another age — fine women, both of them, in the Victorian tradition. In a way they matched their house with its tree-like camellia bushes in the front yard and inside shutters at the windows to keep the sun from fading the red plush and brocade. Alice taught at least two and maybe three generations of Santa Cruzans in her 40-plus years in local schools. Clara was in Santa Cruz a shorter time, as she had married George Taylor and lived in Mountain View and produced a son before she was widowed. The sisters lived quietly, correcting their school papers at the dining table — no one ever sat in the front parlor for mundane purposes. They dressed in somber grays or dull blues or dark browns, and taught the three R's with no nonsense about it. At least Alice did. Just once, in class, the hem of her long skirt misbehaved long enough to give a glimpse of bright green underwear of some kind. Bright green! Imagine. As a third grade mouse, much in awe of teachers and their authority, I never forgot that bright flash. And I have pondered it in later years...so quiet and prim and ladylike she was, but what thwarted, warm, unruly thoughts and passions were buried behind the maiden-lady image? No one will ever know.

Except now, 13 years after they are dead and buried (both in the same year), I find they had fine Spanish blood. And then I remember Alice's dark brown eyes — they had a snap to them. She was born in San Francisco, April 4, 1879, the seventh of eight daughters. Her parents were Edward Halsey and Juana Barbara Wesche (Halsey). Juana was the daughter of Juan Gerardo Wesche, German Consul at Mazatlan, Mexico. Halsey was a son of Judge Charles Halsey, one of San Francisco's first Superior Court judges.

Alice Halsey came to Santa Cruz in 1892 with her mother and stepfather, John Stock. She had graduated from San Jose State in 1899. She started teaching in Grant School, then in 1907 went to Mission Hill School, moving with it to the "new" site at Mission and Storey. She taught until she retired in 1938.

But back in 1910, the parents, John and Juana, both were taken ill and Clara was called back to Santa Cruz to live. The stepfather died first, the mother lived until 1936, and the "girls" taught and took care of her. It was a familiar pattern of life in those days.

*continued on page 95*

Hilda McLean
1974

# Gingerbread House

### 218 Mission Street, Santa Cruz

*Built by Louis Schwartz in 1867 as a rental unit, Gingerbread House was one of "twin" houses, exactly alike. The narrow little house is sided with clapboard shiplap, redwood from Santa Cruz County lumber mills. Note the stickwork in the front gable and the ornate porch railings. Slender turned pillars hold the second story porch with gentle arches between them. In the rear of the house is the modern addition. Gingerbread and its twin are located next to Schwartz's own home which is notable for its elaborately sawn bargeboard, and may be seen in the rear of the photograph. All three houses were built at the same time.*

The Willard Morrises are young people — but they love old houses. One day, while driving down Mission Street, they spied Halsey House.

"If I could ever own a Victorian house, that's the one I want," Willard remarked to his wife.

A few days later they passed it again — and there was a "For Sale" sign on the front lawn. They bought it and moved in. They loved it and enjoyed living there, but it was a bit large for two people. When Gingerbread House, across Mission Street from Halsey House, went up for sale, they bought it too. And now they live in the smaller of the two.

"We had to rewire Gingerbread, and remove some new woodwork that had been nailed in in recent years. We replaced wall moldings with the real old kind that were there originally," Morris explained. "After all, it's 107 years old (in 1974)."

They also removed "new" wallpaper and other recent additions that they felt spoiled the authenticity of the little house.

Gingerbread and its sister twin, were built side by side on 44-foot lots by Louis Schwartz, a Santa Cruz business man. He built a third house, larger, with more "gingerbread" on it for himself. It still stands just a doorstep away. Schwartz rented out the two smaller houses.

Louis Schwartz climbed the ladder of success, rung by rung. A native of Prussia where he was born in 1834, he learned the baking trade, left home at 17 to find work in England, then in New York and finally, in 1854, in California. He arrived on the steamer *Uncle Sam* after crossing the Isthmus, landing in San Francisco with $7 in his pockets. Details are scanty but a year later he was in Santa Cruz to open a merchandise store on Pacific Avenue, in partnership with someone named Brownstone. A year later he dissolved the partnership and had his own store about where the Bubble Bakery is today.

Over the years Schwartz prospered and opened branch stores and lumber yards in San Luis Obispo, Santa Maria and Cayucos. He also had interests in a fleet of ships that carried lumber.

In 1865, shortly before he built his home and two rentals, he married Miss Rebecca Stein. They had eight children, four of whom lived to adulthood.

In later years he was prominent in Santa Cruz Masonic Lodge, Odd Fellows Lodge, Knights of Honor and Knights of Pythias. He also served as a councilman, a director of the Bank of Santa Cruz County and vice president of the Butchers' Union of Santa Cruz.

Mr. Schwartz's motto was "What has been done can be done." He is buried in the Jewish Cemetery located off Meder Street. Today his three houses are much admired by connoisseurs of Victoriana.

Next door in Gingerbread's twin, at 214 Mission Street, where she has lived for years, is Carmen Guichard of another pioneer family. She still uses a little wood stove for heat, and raises most of her vegetables in the backyard.

# Haslam House

### 304 Walnut Avenue,
### Santa Cruz

*A modified Queen Anne style with many elaborate "fishscale" shingles. The boxed cornices are frieze decorated, the Queen Anne tower has a finial. The house was built in 1893 on what was one of the most stylish streets in town. However, its location served two purposes: in addition to "style," its owner could walk to work from there, and did. Built of local redwood, the house has parlor, living room, dining room, entry hall, office, three bedrooms on the second floor, and baths; a full attic and a handsome oak staircase. In recent years, while being used as an antique shop, the front porch was closed in with glass panels. Only the kitchen and baths have been modernized by Dr. and Mrs. Estess, present owners, who have furnished the house with elegant antiques of the Victorian period.*

Framed in large trees, one of them the "monkey tree" that was so popular in Santa Cruz around the turn of the century, a pale green Queen Anne house rises to full majestic height at the corner of Walnut Avenue and Chestnut Street.

Haslam House was built in 1893, designed by architect E.L. Van Cleek. J.B. Dawson was the contractor. The house cost $4,500.

Well preserved, the house was used as an antique shop for eight years before Dr. and Mrs. Floyd Estess purchased it in 1968 and restored it to its full Victorian splendor.

W.D. Haslam was born in Santa Cruz in 1860, grew up and graduated from Santa Cruz High School in 1879. Two years before that date, his father died, and young William Douglass Haslam found himself with his mother and sister to support.

He sold newspapers at 50 cents a week; he did odd jobs at Cooper's Store on the corner of Front and Cooper Streets. When an offer of a good job in Oakland came to him, he left Santa Cruz for three years to work in William C. Mason's grocery store. From Oakland, young Haslam went to Bodie to serve as private secretary to the superintendent of the Standard Consolidated Mining Company.

Haslam credited his rapid rise to this position of greater responsibility to his friendship with William Willis, a mining secretary. Of Willis he always said in later years: "His example, instruction and influence were invaluable, and his business methods I have never seen excelled. Many times daily matters come up now in my business to which his principles and methods are applied."

By the time William Haslam made that somewhat stilted statement, he was cashier and secretary of Santa Cruz City Bank and City Savings Bank.

He also became one of the incorporators and directors of the East Santa Cruz Railway Company. As for social life, Haslam is reported to have been very "fond of social life," and he was a prominent member of the Masonic Lodge and the Native Sons of the Golden West Lodge.

Haslam's mother married again, was widowed again, and his sister, Bessie G. Haslam, was able to attend San Jose State Normal School (San Jose State University), thanks to her brother's business acumen. She graduated in 1890.

Three years later the graceful house was built on Walnut Avenue. Walnut, in those days, according to one old time Santa Cruzan, was "the" place to live.

Willie Haslam made it — and the whole town took off its hat to him. From Harrison's *History of Santa Cruz* (1893): "For many years there was a struggle against straightened (sic) circumstances, and the boy's mental and moral muscles were rendered staunch and true by that best of all discipline, the effort to aid those we love."

CYNTHIA MATHEWS

# The Twelfth Mission — Santa Cruz

The story of Santa Cruz Mission has everything: love, hate, success and failure, pathos and bathos. The first structure was a rude shelter of wood slats stuck into the ground, probably with a thatched roof, and it stood not "up on the hill" but "down in the flat." The exact site is not known. But from the temporary crude hut, came the move up onto Mission Hill and the building of the full-fledged mission. Most importantly, it was safe from the flooding San Lorenzo River.

The original mission was built by the Franciscan padres and their Indian neophytes and it was composed of stone and adobe, 112 feet long, topped first with thatch, then later with tiles. The mission was 30 feet wide and its walls were 25 feet high, constructed of stone to a height of three feet, then adobe to the eaves.

This mission had everything in its favor: rich crop lands, a fine water supply, stone and lumber resources and Indians to do the work.

The padres and their charges worked hard: an orchard was put in, grain fields and vegetable crops were planted; a water-powered grist mill was installed; adjoining adobe buildings were put up to house soldiers, weaving looms, blacksmith shop, storerooms, leather-working, offices and priests' quarters. By 1797 there were 644 souls counted as saved.

But that was a fateful year. Villa de Branciforte, a civil settlement, was established just across the San Lorenzo River. The Villa was an easy-going place where bear and bull fights and horse-racing went on, even on Sunday, accompanied by fandangoes, gambling and drinking. Fun was more popular than work and church, over at the Villa. The mission padres fought a losing battle against its pleasures, in trying to keep their Indian neophytes to the straight and narrow. And other problems followed.

By 1800 the Indian population was down to 492 due to disease and death or desertion. In 1812 one of the priests was lured out into the orchard and murdered. In 1818 a French pirate, de Bouchard, threatened to land his ship at Santa Cruz and sack the mission. Due to rough weather at sea, he didn't land, but the priests at Mission Santa Cruz panicked and fled over the mountains with their Indian neophytes. In going, they turned the mission over to Villa officials to guard.

The Villa officials guarded it so well that much of it disappeared forever — including barrels of wine and other supplies.

In 1834-35 the final blow fell: the mission was secularized, and turned over to Villa authorities for good. Mission properties valued at $50,000 seemed to evaporate into thin air. Herds dwindled. The mission buildings fell into crumbling ruins, helped along by heavy rain storms and earthquakes.

But Holy Cross Catholic Church rose again on a site very near that of the original mission chapel. In 1853 Santa Cruz was restored as a mission church; in 1858 a wood sanctuary was built. The present brick church was built in 1889.

The mission replica was built in 1932. It follows the design of the original mission faithfully, and is about one-half as large. Mrs. Gladys Sullivan Doyle gave money that made its construction possible.

*Original Mission Santa Cruz was built 1793-94; last vestiges were demolished in 1889. Replica was built in 1931.*

# Alice's House

### 127 Green Street,
### Santa Cruz

Residents of Green Street in Santa Cruz feel they have something special...it is the kind of street that contributes to Santa Cruz' charm and unique "New England" atmosphere.

The street has another big plus factor, according to residents. "We like the idea of living so near the central shopping district and yet we are apart from it," comments Mrs. Geraldine Work who owns and lives in "Alice's House."

The basic form of her house is Victorian Gothic Revival, but the entrance, the windows and the house's balanced symmetry point to Greek Revival. It was built before 1870, probably by one Otis A. Longley.

The "Alice" was Alice Farnham, daughter of Enoch George Farnham who bought the house and property from Silas Randall in 1878. Alice was Farnham's only child and she left her mark on the house. Scratched into one of the old, bubble-glass windows are the initials: A.E.F. — Alice Edith Farnham. She also planted the huge Belle of Portugal rose at the corner of the front porch.

Mr. Farnham operated a hay, grain and feed store in partnership with A.P. Swanton, and Alice was 11 years old when the family settled on Green Street.

Another street, of which there is just a tiny portion left, Crossing Street, ran from Green through to School Street. Green Street itself was, in early days, the main thoroughfare that led up and over Mission Hill, connecting the downtown "flat" with the Potrero north of it on present-day River Street. Instead of the extension of North Pacific which skirts the chalk rock bluff of Mission Hill, a waterfall cascaded over that same bluff to form a pool at its base, from which it flowed into the San Lorenzo River.

Green Street's name is something of a mystery. It was named for a man named Green who donated lumber for the first Methodist Church building which was located on the south-east corner of Green and Mission Streets. There was an E.G. Green whose wife was active in the WCTU, a J.S. Green who lived on Washington Street, and a John D. Green. In fact there were so many Greens in early-day California that a noted historian threw up his hands, figuratively speaking, and gave up trying to get them all straight.

We do know that John D. Green came to Santa Cruz in 1847, married Lydia Hitchcock and bought "Crazy" Wright's sawmill in 1849 for $2,000. The sawmill was located at Rincon, up the San Lorenzo canyon, and is said to have furnished lumber for the First Methodist sanctuary. Chances are good that Green Street was named for John D.

In the intervening years, Alice's House, with her initials on the window and her rose thriving on the front porch, has been lived in — and cherished — by Mrs. Work who retired three years ago as Santa Cruz City-County Librarian.

# Baldwin House

### 425 Locust Street, Santa Cruz

*There is something faintly Gothic about this plain little house at 425 Locust Street. Perhaps "Carpenter Gothic" would be a better term. Yet its simple lines have worn well down through the years since it was built about 1880. It is of redwood, shiplap siding, with pierced posts holding its porch roof.*

For more than 90 years a member of the Baldwin family has lived at 425 Locust Street in Santa Cruz.

The little pioneer frame house has sheltered a passing parade of weddings, births, funerals, family get-togethers, meetings of "THE Club" and just plain everyday living.

A member of the family lives there still — Miss Ruth Baldwin.

The early-day Baldwin family was a friendly tangle of "kissing cousins". Levi K. Baldwin was first to come West from Massachusetts where he had been a prosperous farmer until business reverses wiped him out. Levi was a generous man. He endorsed mortgages for several desperate friends; the mortgages fell due and Levi found himself forced to mortgage his own home in order to meet the notes.

In 1858 he and his wife came to California via the Isthmus of Panama, settling first in Marin County where he operated a dairy. In 1872 he moved to Santa Cruz to start another dairy which became famous for its butter. He developed the business from his original purchase of 157 acres and 23 cows to 1,700 acres and 400 cows. And in Santa Cruz he regained the wealth and prestige he had lost in the East.

Levi became president of Santa Cruz County Bank in the 1890's, and before that he served as a county supervisor.

In 1898 he bought his house on Locust Street from Harrison Terry who had built it a few years before. When Levi died, the house went to his daughter, May, and in 1906 May deeded the property to Carrie Baldwin, a cousin. When Carrie died in 1953, the house passed to her daughter Ruth who lives there yet.

Ruth's memories are many and colorful of the passing parade of Baldwins and their friends who gathered in the little house. Her sister, Elizabeth Amy Baldwin, was married there in 1904 to Leslie J. Wright. The family was living there in that year, renting at the time.

"The parlor was hung with smilax and roses," she recalls. "The dining room was decorated with geraniums. I was just a small girl at the time, but I was allowed to greet the guests and take the men's hats."

Ruth also remembers THE Club, to which her mother belonged. Widows of all the best families were members. At intervals the stately and well-fed widows would get their black silks out of mothballs, meet at each other's homes and have dinner (luncheon today) and a social afternoon.

Favorite meat loaf recipes were cooked up, pickles were unjarred, apple pies perfumed the air. And then the parade of ladies in long, rustling black silk gowns would begin. Ruth was official greeter.

"My how that child has grown. Carrie, why don't you put a brick on her head?" They always said it. It was a sort of left-handed compliment to Carrie's care and feeding of her smallest daughter.

After dinner, if a certain Mrs. Faye left early, the other ladies would play Dutch Whist — Mrs. Faye considered Whist to be a contrivance of the devil himself. If Mrs. Faye stayed, the ladies chatted, looked through the stereopticon or perhaps enjoyed a bit of music.

*continued on page 96*

# The Octagonal Gem

Corner of Cooper and Front
Streets, Santa Cruz

On March 11, 1882, Santa Cruz County Board of Supervisors began advertising for plans for a "Hall of Records" building. On April 8 of the same year, drawings and specifications for an octagonal brick building were presented to the Board. The octagon shape was said to be taken from a $50 octagonal-shaped gold piece minted in San Francisco in 1851-52.

Architects of the 19th Century seem to have been intrigued with the octagon shape; there were a number of such buildings in California, few of which remain today. A.W. Burrill was the architect for Santa Cruz' Hall of Records. When bids were opened, lowest one for $10,470 came from the California Bridge Company. But the Santa Cruz County "fathers" drove a hard bargain; they insisted the bid be reduced to an even $10,000 before they would give the go-ahead. They also stipulated that the building be completed in four months.

The cornerstone-laying took place June 10, 1882, with Santa Cruz Masonic Lodge officiating and Governor George C. Perkins of California as the main guest of honor. Wood seats were hastily built to accommodate the crowds. The ceremony was followed by a dance with a five-piece orchestra tootling and thumping out tunes such as "Darling Nellie Gray" and "Listen to the Mocking Bird."

Gentlemen in swallow-tails and ladies in high button shoes and pastel silk gowns swooped and dashed about the dance floor in genteel fashion — probably in the old Armory where most of the big parties were held.

Three months later, on September 9, 1882, County Supervisors graciously allowed Burrill and the construction company one more month to finish the building.

On October 7, 1882, the finished octagon was turned over to the County and a warrant was drawn to pay for it. The unique brick building served Santa Cruz County as its Hall of Records for 86 years although the last two or three decades were punctuated with cries for "more room." In the early 1920's an ugly brick appendage was added to the Front Street side in an attempt to provide needed space.

When the County began to build a new Governmental Center for itself, people who had passed the old octagon for years without really seeing it, began to take a second look. The building's rarity and architectural importance had been taken for granted for years.

When demolition rumors began to fly about, a few people began to work for its preservation. The demolition rumors even reached the historically tuned ears of Donald C. Biggs, director of the California Historical Society at that time. He had led the battle to save Portsmouth Plaza and the San Francisco Mint. And he was just as concerned about the impending loss of Santa Cruz' octagon.

In February, 1968, Santa Cruz County Board of Supervisors passed a resolution preserving the brick octagon as a County Museum. With the aid of a historic preservation grant from HUD, U.S. Department of Housing and Urban Development, the restoration was carried out and the Museum was dedicated June 17, 1972.

1882 RECORDS

Hulda McLean 1974

# The Newer
# Baldwin House

### 425 Locust Street,
### Santa Cruz

*Built in 1908, modified Queen Anne.*

"Jack of all trades, master of none..." That old saying did not hold true for F.D. Baldwin.

It is true that he tried a variety of occupations, but he finally settled on dairying and became prosperous enough to retire to the large home he built on Locust Street.

However, before he retired, he took on the operation of a large apple orchard in the Pajaro Valley, was elected Santa Cruz County Supervisor and served two terms, was named chairman of the County Republican Central Committee, helped frame the Santa Cruz City Charter, and was made a director of the City Bank of Santa Cruz and the City Savings Bank.

Baldwin was born in Massachusetts in 1847, grew up there and became a school teacher. He was born a bit too late for the Gold Rush which brought many New Englanders rushing to California. But by 1867 he had heard enough about "Go West, young man!" to whet his interest. He came to California and settled in Marin County where he taught school for several years. While teaching he cast an appraising eye at a Marin dairy business and got into it. In two years he moved to Monterey County, returned for a brief visit to his home state, then came west again. This time he tried mining in the Mother Lode; that lasted about a year.

He returned to teaching, first in Placer County, then in Monterey County where he ran a dairy on the side. The dairying became so profitable that he went into it full-time, five years in Watsonville, and 18 in Santa Cruz. In 1873 he had somehow found time to marry Mary A. Race and they had three children: Grace, who became a teacher; Arnold, who became Santa Cruz County Surveyor, and Roscoe, who farmed the Pajaro orchard.

His home, built after the turn of the century, nevertheless reflects an earlier era with its rounded cupola, bow windows and carriage house in the backyard. In the soft bitumen paving of the driveway, one can yet see the prints of horses' hooves, left over from carriage days.

Out in the backyard, next to the carriage house, stands the original Baldwin home, built in the 1860's. It stood originally at the front of the property but was moved back to make way for the more elaborate Baldwin house.

Even old age didn't slow F.D. Baldwin to any great extent. He became president of both banks, and retained his desk in the bank office after it had merged and become a part of the Bank of Italy, and finally, the Bank of America.

Neighbors of his on Locust Street were familiar with the sight of the frail old man, age 96, being wheeled in his wicker wheelchair on his way downtown to the bank he served so proudly for so many years.

54

# Blackburn House

### Cedar and Sycamore Streets, Santa Cruz

*Built about 1851-59 by Judge William Blackburn for whom Blackburn Gulch and Blackburn Street are named, the house is a Greek Revival [1850's-1860], with plain boxed cornices and shiplap siding. The house is located at 152 Center Street but is best viewed from the junction of Cedar and Sycamore which it faces. It is now the home and office of the owner of the Smart Motel.*

Judge William Blackburn stood for no nonsense. In his zealous pursuit of early-day justice in Santa Cruz, he often brought down on himself some sharp rebukes from higher-ups. But the people of Santa Cruz admired and respected the old boy. And when he ordered a close haircut for a troublesome teenager of 1847, the town had a good laugh. The teenager had sheared the tail and mane from a Spaniard's fine riding horse. In Judge Blackburn's opinion (an eye for an eye and a tooth for a tooth), the teenage boy was sheared — in public. Right in front of the Judge's office, in fact.

The Judge was known as a "character" — and a man not to fool with. A native of Virginia, he came to Alta California in 1845 with the Swasey-Todd Party. He was a cabinet-maker by trade, but there weren't many cabinets being made then in California. And he had to eat. So he settled in Zayante to make shingles. In 1846 the shingle-maker joined the California Bear Flag Battalion under Captain John C. Fremont and marched to the Battle of Buenaventura. After the excitement of trying to capture Alta California for the United States, Blackburn came back to settle in Santa Cruz. He opened a hotel and store on Holy Cross Plaza which was the center of town in those days, in a two-story adobe building called the "Eagle Hotel." He also was appointed Alcalde of Santa Cruz — hence his career as "Judge."

By 1848 the energetic Judge was building a sawmill out on Branciforte Creek in a gulch still known as Blackburn Gulch — when gold was discovered in California. He resigned his alcaldeship and rushed to the gold fields. He didn't stay long. He seemed to feel there was gold — of a surer variety — right back in Santa Cruz. In 1849 he was back in town and was appointed Justice of the Peace under Territorial Government.

In 1851 the Judge settled down on the flat between Pacific Avenue and Neary Lagoon. It was about that time that he built the fine old house which still stands there today. Blackburn's brothers came out west to join their brother, and Daniel went to farming in partnership with his Judge brother. The potato boom was on — miners were hungry for them — and in one year the two brothers cleared about $100,000 on potatoes grown in the rich bottomland acres. Judge Blackburn sent potatoes weighing as much as four pounds apiece to the Crystal Palace Fair in New York and won top prizes.

In 1859, when he was 45 years old, the busy Judge took time out to marry Harriet Mead. The wedding took place in the home of Harriet's brother-in-law and sister, Dr. and Mrs. J.C. Kittredge. The home still stands at the tip of Beach Hill, known as the Hotel Mc-Cray.

By the 1860's Judge William Blackburn was recognized as Santa Cruz' richest citizen. Everything he touched seemed to turn to gold.

And yet for him, the 1860's ended in sadness. He lost his only child, a two-year-old son, in 1864, and the Judge himself died three years later in March, 1867.

Down through the years since, the Judge's fertile acreage has been gradually covered with streets, homes, a railroad depot and train tracks.

# Hollins House,
# Pasatiempo

Pasatiempo Golf Club,
Santa Cruz

*Upper photo: The Hollins House shortly after completion with the panoramic view enjoyed from it.*

*Lower photo: The Hollins House shortly after it had been landscaped.*

This story starts with a dream and a fortune and a pre-Women's Libber who had them — and lost them. Marion Hollins had the world at her fingertips the day she rode her horse over a 600-acre property that had been part of the Mexican Land Grant, Rancho Carbonero. It was the late 1920's. She was the nation's top woman golfer in 1921, an accomplished horsewoman, an all-round athlete, and she had made a fortune investing in the fabulous Kettleman Oil Fields.

Her dream was to develop one of the nation's finest golf courses and country clubs, on the rolling hills of the old Mexican Rancho property overlooking Monterey Bay.

Marion bought the property and hired Dr. Alistair MacKenzie, internationally famous advisor to such golf clubs as the Royal and Ancient St. Andrews and Royal St. George. He laid out the plan for the 18-hole course. The Olmstead Brothers of Boston mapped the general plan for the property which was to include homesites, nine miles of road, tennis courts, six miles of bridle paths and a clubhouse. It was to be called Pasatiempo Country Club and Estates, the "Pasatiempo" for "pastime."

A jury composed of club directors and several architects passed judgment on all proposed building plans. The first three homes and the caddy house were the work of William W. Wurster of San Francisco. One of the houses, Marion Hollins' own, posed some unusual problems, as she would not allow a single tree to be cut or removed from the steep hillside lot.

Clarence Tantau of San Francisco was selected as a juror and as the architect for the Clubhouse — actually the third building used as a clubhouse, as the ranch house near the gate was the first, and a second also was built. Tantau made an extensive study of the early California dwelling, visiting smaller towns and historic buildings throughout the State. In 1937 his clubhouse was completed...and a magazine of that year describes it, "...True to the historic as well as to the geographic background of the place, his design delights in its simplicity and charm..."

The golf course had opened on September 8, 1929, with 300 guests, members of the great and glittering "400", the jet set of the 1920's, watching a golf match starring Marion Hollins, Bobby Jones, Glenda Collett and Cyril Tolley.

On March 15, 1931, one of the five annual meets of the Pacific Coast Steeplechase and Racing Association opened the new steeplechase course at Pasatiempo. Not even the great depression kept "society" from entering its finest horses in the event. On September 5, 1937, Pasatiempo's new swimming pool was opened with a big social splash. Among the famous guests was Mary Pickford — remember? The Clubhouse had been completed shortly before the pool, and activities centered there with a dinner-dance to the music of Jimmy James and his Pasatiempo Country Club Orchestra. The Clubhouse, with its 50-foot living room, was filled to capacity for the party.

Plans were then announced for the opening of a Polo Field in mid-October with "spectacular play for the Governor's cup trophy."

"It is under the directing genius of 'this great character' as Marion Hollins is called by all who know her, that Pasatiempo has won its

*continued on page 96*

# An Extravagant Apartment House

High Street and Highland Avenue, Santa Cruz

*This impressive Mission Revival apartment house was built in 1912 with William Bray as the architect. When built it was described as "Moorish in design, with an elaborate interior court with fountain." It contains 50 rooms, and is located at the northeast corner of High Street at Highland Avenue. Especially notable are its twin towers, and its twin espadanas which are decorated with variations of the quatrefoil.*

Santa Cruzans sat up and took notice in 1912 when they heard that a 50-room apartment house was to be built.

Piedmont Court was built on a silver dream which vanished like a will-o'-the-wisp before the court was finished. The building was to cost $50,000, was to be of Moorish design and would boast an elaborate inner court with a fountain.

Originator of all these fancy ideas (for that day, in Santa Cruz), was a wealthy native of Sonora, Mexico, Don Pedro Chisem. Don Pedro "discovered" Santa Cruz about 144 years after the first Spanish explorers marched through. But, as with each new "discoverer," he believed he had found a truly unique place. He was impressed with the climate, the beauty of the town on Monterey Bay, and the financial possibilities. He also brought to town a wallet bulging with Mexican banknotes, money which came from his interests in silver mines.

No expense was spared to create the finest apartment house in town. It was to be fireproof, modern, built of concrete, with steam heat, electricity and hot and cold running water throughout.

Now this was in a day when most Santa Cruzans still heated their homes with wood fires, many pumped water by hand, and even more answered nature's calls in a backyard "telephone booth." Local citizens were understandably impressed with Don Pedro's plans.

Work began in August, 1912, and the graceful structure began to rise at the corner of High Street and Highland Avenue. John Church superintended the construction. George Cardiff supplied cement and T.F. Costella was in charge of all cement work.

While Piedmont Court was going up, Don Pedro moved his family here and bought the old Farmers' Union Building which was located where Santa Cruz Bank of America stands today. He had plans for building a four-story hotel and business block there.

Then disaster struck in the form of political upheavals in Mexico. Don Pedro's silver mines no longer filled his wallet to overflowing. The silver flood dwindled to a drip, then to nothing at all. He returned to Mexico to try to prime the silver pump and restore his fortunes. But his ventures in Santa Cruz were at an end.

Stately Piedmont Court was completed with money put up by Frank G. Wilson and Bruce Sharpe, local businessmen. The court was finished and for years was "the" place for apartment dwellers.

In 1952 the handsome building was purchased by the California Retired Teachers Association. They gave it the name "Calreta Court," and today Don Pedro's handsome Mission-style apartment house is home to a group of retired educators.

# The Tragic Cowells Lived Here

Tragedy and a despotic patriarch ruled the lives of the five Cowell children: they were not to marry, suitors could only be after the family fortune.

One wonders, looking at the old home, today, if it ever rang to the sound of laughter and youthful fun. The house was built by Albion P. Jordan, Santa Cruz' pioneer lime industrialist who came to the county in 1853. He established a partnership with Isaac E. Davis, the lime business flourished, and in 1865 Jordan sold his share and his home to Henry Cowell.

Henry Cowell was the first man to ship cement from Belgium and fire brick from England to California. He had the Midas touch — everything turned to gold. He also had his ideas of how life should be lived. And it didn't include marriage for his five children.

One son, Ernest, rebelled and wed without parental blessings. He was ostracized — then reinstated when he broke with his wife. Ernest was the Cowell who left $250,000 to University of California for construction of Cowell Infirmary on the Berkeley Campus.

Henry Cowell, founder and patriarch, came to Santa Cruz in 1865. He and his wife Alice had five children: Isabella, Ernest, Samuel H., Helen and Agnes. Samuel H. was known as Harry, and it was he who spent the most time at the family's Santa Cruz ranch. Cowell interests were widespread; there were great ranches in many parts of California as well as the huge lime and cement operation.

Patriarch Cowell was able to buy the other half of the Davis-Jordan lime interests in 1888 when Isaac E. Davis died, and from the nucleus of the Santa Cruz operation, he built the family fortune.

In 1897 the Cowells moved from Santa Cruz, bag and baggage, to San Francisco. Their mansion was located at 2610 Jackson Street.

Six years later tragedy came upon the family. Henry Cowell, father of the clan, died. And Agnes, the youngest daughter, was killed on the Santa Cruz Ranch. She had come down to spend a day or so, and went out to pick wild flowers; it was May and they were blooming in the meadows and fields of the Cowell acreage. Agnes took a horse and buggy — a high-spirited horse she had been warned against using. She and the Cowell housekeeper set out across the fields, a buggy wheel struck a rock, the horse bolted and Agnes was thrown from the buggy. She died of a broken neck.

The Cowells sent a special railroad train to Santa Cruz to carry Agnes back to San Francisco for burial. And as a result of the accident, Isabella never set foot in Santa Cruz again. She and the other sister, Helen, lived as recluses on one of the family estates at Atherton. When Helen died in 1932, Isabella moved out and had a bulldozer come in and flatten their Atherton home. She left it that way — smashed in collapsed ruins, and went to San Francisco to live with her brother Harry.

Harry was the rancher and horseman of the family. He became engaged once, to a cousin, Edith Lane. However, the Cowell family broke that up too and Harry never married. He died on February 1, 1955, in the San Francisco mansion, after making a gift of 1,623 acres of his Santa Cruz County property for Henry Cowell Redwoods State Park. It is named for his father, the old patriarch.

*In 1964, before he died, George Cardiff, who worked for the Cowell family for many years, estimated that the original part of the Cowell Ranch home at Santa Cruz was from 110 to 112 years old. The oldest part of the house contains the kitchen with its huge fireplace, reminiscent of New England homes where a black iron pot of beans or stew was always bubbling over the fire. In later years, rooms were added onto what is the front of the house today, probably by the Cowells, who lived there from 1865 to 1897. The house is simple in style, resembling the California adobe to a degree, with redwood siding and slender square posts holding its front porch roof.*

# Palaise Monte Carlo also known as Golden Gate Villa

924 Third Street,
Santa Cruz

*Perhaps the finest example in Santa Cruz of Queen Anne style, this elegant house was built in 1891. T.J. Welch was the architect. Originally the third floor tower, or belvedere, was open, with arched openings and columns. It was enclosed in recent years, and that is the most noticeable change that has been made. The house cost about $20,000 to build, even in those days. It contains many fine stained glass windows, elephant hide on walls of one room, an onyx fireplace and some gold-plated lighting fixtures. Original painting and decorating was done by Fraser and Keefe of San Francisco. The house has six chimneys and 22 rooms. Windows in some rooms depict fruits, flowers, and musical instruments. The largest stained glass window on the stair landing is said to be Agnes, tragic daughter of the house, and it also is said that strands of her hair were embedded in the glass when it was made.*

She's a "grande dame" in the finest tradition.

She has come out of a tragic past into a sparkling future. She's the Palais Monte Carlo, sometimes known as the McLaughlin House when associated with the tragedy, sometimes referred to as Golden Gate Villa.

The fine old Beach Hill mansion is one of Santa Cruz' best examples of the "Elegant 90's." Major Frank W. McLaughlin, who had the house built in 1891, would feel right at home there today, so beautifully has it been restored. So would his step-daughter, Agnes, whom he shot to death as she lay sleeping in a bedroom upstairs. And so would the Major's wife, who had died two years before, November 16, 1905, on the exact date he shot Agnes and drank a poison cocktail.

A bon vivant who lived well and entertained on a lavish scale, the Major couldn't face poverty, either for himself or for his step-daughter, Agnes. Carefully and deliberately he planned the murder and suicide. Several months before the fateful date, November 16, 1907, he wrote 15 farewell letters, a few filled with detailed instructions and last requests.

And then the day came — the anniversary of the death of his wife. The Major took his revolver in hand, went into Agnes' room, put it to her temple and pulled the trigger. She lived for a few hours — not many. He then drank cyanide. Before he died he went to the telephone and called Lt. Governor William Jeter, a close and old friend. He told Jeter what he had done. By the time Jeter got to the big house on Beach Hill, the Major was dead.

Friend of Presidents, Kings and political greats, he couldn't face poverty.

The Major had had a fabulous career before his run of bad luck began. In 1878 he was in Newark, N.J., connected with the Edison Phonograph Company and a close friend of Thomas Alva Edison. Major McLaughlin built a nine-mile tunnel for the Big Bend Project; he built a 30-mile flume for the Miocene Hydraulic Mine and huge siphons for the United States Hydraulic Mine at Cherokee. All this brought him fame and fortune — before he came west to Oroville and the "Great Chinese Wall Folly."

The Major dreamed up a plan to divert the Feather River to harvest the crop of gold nuggets he believed existed in the river bed. No one bothered to tell him that 40-odd years before, that had been done by gold rushers.

The Major went to work, Thomas Edison came out to string up lights so work could go on around the clock; wealthy Britishers sank fortunes into the project which was to culminate with the harnessing of the river to develop a huge electric plant. And then — the fateful day came in 1897 when the entire project blew up in the Major's face. The two-mile stone wall, dam and spillway were abandoned. The Major came to Santa Cruz to live in lonely splendor in his big house. His wife died, he grieved and brooded — until that day in 1907.

A group of 35 people attended the Major's funeral which was held in the house. His and Agnes' bodies were sent East for burial by Sam Ricker, who had been engaged to Agnes.

*continued on page 97*

Hilda McLean 1974

# Cooper House

## 110 Cooper Street, Santa Cruz

*Built in 1894-95, Cooper House was designed by Comstock and constructed by Thomas Beck. A Richardson Romanesque Revival building, it is said to be one of only two or three of its kind west of the Mississippi. When it was built it was considered very advanced for a town the size of Santa Cruz. It is constructed of sand mold brick, with brownstone brick facing. Of particular note are the arched brick ceilings of the basement. Remodeling for present shop purposes has changed the interior to a degree. The graceful double staircase, long closed up and unused by the County, was opened up and restored to use by Max Walden, present owner. The carved rail was duplicated, also the original iron work. Much stained glass has been added inside, a pleasing change in decor.*

Cooper House, before it became the home of a number of boutique shops and a restaurant, was Santa Cruz County's fifth courthouse.

The County did its business — or most of it — there, until growing pains drove it out in 1967, and into the newly-completed Governmental Center on the bank of the San Lorenzo River.

Cooper House, a handsome building constructed of "gold" bricks, was in danger of demolition for a while, after the County moved out. Its fate hung in the balance for a few months with many old-timers urging its preservation — people like former County Recorder Lela Swasey and Santa Cruz artist Lillian Huebner. They wrote letters and buttonholed anyone who would listen — and a few who wouldn't. Downtown Santa Cruz was sick, economically. There were more than a dozen empty stores in the three main blocks. There were those citizens who felt that a tall new building of some sort should go in on the former courthouse lot.

Then, in a move that was later proclaimed a stroke of genius by some, and something else by others, the late Chuck Abbott brought to town a man named Max Walden. Walden had masterminded the highly successful Old Town rehabilitation shopping center in Los Gatos. He took one look at the forlorn old courthouse building and couldn't stand to turn his back on it. He bought it and took on what has probably developed into the greatest challenge of his life. It cost $75,000.

Today, a great many dollars and much work later, the old courthouse is Cooper House, named for the highly esteemed Cooper brothers, William and John, who donated the land on which the County built its first and second "real" Courthouses. By that is meant the first Courthouses that were built for *that* purpose.

The very first Courthouse business was conducted in the Eagle Hotel on the Mission Plaza, an old Mexican adobe. Santa Cruz County was created on February 18, 1850. Two years later, the new county paid Thomas Fallon the then handsome sum of $3,500 for his combination home and store, also on the upper Plaza. By 1860, when it was becoming obvious that the main business of the Town was all down "on the flat," (where it is today), the County moved its headquarters into the brick Flatiron Building, second floor. The city fathers stayed there until 1867. In that year, a new brick Courthouse was built on the land given for that purpose by John and William Cooper. That Courthouse burned in the great fire of April 14, 1894, and the present Cooper House was then built as the County's second "real" Courthouse, on the same site.

Gone were the days when the City fathers made do with leaky roofs over their heads, tattered ledgers to write the County's business in and maybe a hen's quill for the writing. Sophistication entered the scene with the first brick Courthouse, the one that burned. It cost $20,000 — an unbelievable sum in 1867.

The Coopers, who established one of the first downtown mercantile stores, were civic-minded citizens. William particularly, has gone down in history as a man who befriended the bewildered and destitute Mission Indians who had nowhere to turn when the Santa Cruz Mission closed down. He fed them, gave them blankets and

*continued on page 97*

# Santa Cruz City Hall

When Santa Cruz began to outgrow the old Hihn mansion, which served as its City Hall until 1937, the city fathers began to think about building a new City Hall on the same site.

The Hihn property had originally reached from Walnut Avenue, at the present Santa Cruz High School property, north to Locust Street and east to Vine Street. (Vine today is Cedar.) The property near Walnut, was used as the Hihn pasture — everyone in those days had a family cow, and two or three horses to pull the family buggy, surrey or wagon.

Center Street did not go through in those days, when Mr. Hihn sold another portion of his land for the site of Santa Cruz Public Library.

Mrs. Therese Hihn, widowed in 1913, lived on in the huge old Hihn mansion until her death on April 20, 1919. The City of Santa Cruz purchased and used the mansion from 1923 to 1937 as its City Hall.

When this was considered no longer feasible, a plan was drawn up by C.J. Ryland for a new City Hall to be built in three sections; a northerly wing on Locust Street, a central section, and a south wing on Church Street. It was to be one-story, with a porch around the U-shaped courtyard for which a fountain was planned.

The architectural style is Monterey Colonial Revival.

Funds for the City Hall were secured through the efforts of U.S. Senator William Gibbs McAdoo and Congressman John J. McGrath.

The old Hihn mansion was demolished to make way for the new City Hall which served well for nearly 30 years. Then in 1965, once again faced with the problem of adequate space for its growing departments, the City of Santa Cruz had plans drawn for an addition to the City Hall. Robert Stevens Associates designed a two-story structure which was placed to the rear, or West, of the existing City Hall. Architecturally it is a pleasing and well-designed part of the whole.

The first new City Hall building cost $144,857 of which the Federal Government paid about $60,000 and the Santa Cruz Rifle Club paid $140. The Spanish gardens, which are universally admired and commented on, initially cost $9,800. The recent addition to City Hall cost $300,000 and added 10,000 square feet of space.

There are two fountains splashing and flowers blooming almost all year 'round, at Santa Cruz City Hall.

# Johnston House

### 245 Ocean View Avenue, Santa Cruz

*Special notice should be taken of this somewhat severe Eastlake style house, for its interiors and details. The foyer floor is original, metal wainscoting and virgin redwood interior trim are retained, and the 12-foot sliding doors are of cherry and redwood. The terrace railing is from the old Garibaldi Hotel and a modern window, which had been installed on the south side of the house, has been removed and the original exterior restored. A previous owner had closed a second floor front porch but luckily saved and used the old arches and railings. Much of the recent restoration work has been done by Kenneth M. Bryant, a local contractor who searched out appropriate old lumber for the purpose. The photograph shows a group, unknown but probably that of the Arthur Cotton family, having a tea party on the front lawn. The old "pie crust" trim around the tower was removed long ago. When built, Johnston House was the twin of Smith House which is across the street from it, identical as to tower, trim and all.*

The property on which this Eastlake style house stands, first came into modern California records in June of 1864 when titles were being settled in the Village and Town of Branciforte. Villa de Branciforte was a separate entity, not a part of the City of Santa Cruz until 1907. This division dated back to Santa Cruz Mission days when the town of Santa Cruz grew up around the Mission, and Villa de Branciforte was established as a separate civil settlement by the Spaniards.

The property that today includes Ocean View Avenue, was awarded in 1864 to Francesco and Guadalupe Sorio, thus disposing of an old Spanish Land Grant, or a portion of it, within the California legal structure.

The Sorios sold to Mrs. Martha Wilson in 1870 and it has been said that this house was built for her shortly afterward, although Mrs. Wilson is said to have built and lived in another house a short distance from this one. (See Page   ). There were nearly 13 acres of land in the parcel the Sorios sold.

But the house is more appropriately called Johnston House, and an article from the *Santa Cruz Surf*, November of 1891, bears out the fact that A. M. Johnston built it.

"The Beautiful House Just Finished for A.M. Johnston...a leading merchant of this city. The symmetry and architectural beauty of the exterior, the comfort, elegance and completeness of the interior, and the magnificence of the views to be had from every window and porch, ranks this among the first of the handsome homes of Santa Cruz..."

The article goes on to describe various parts of the house. It had an entrance hall, front parlor, back parlor, dining room, a small library ("Mr. Johnston's fine collection of books already fills the shelves entirely"), a kitchen lauded as "one of the largest and most convenient rooms in the house with ample closets, a modern sink finished with a tiled front, and all the conveniences a thrifty housekeeper could wish for." A side porch contained a lavatory with "hot and cold water."

On the second floor there were four large bedrooms, a bathroom, a laundry chute to the basement laundry room. The second floor was reached by two stairways, one front stair, more elegant with polished rail and woodwork, and a smaller back stair for the help. The attic extended over the entire house and was unfinished except for — the enchanting tower room!

It was described as "a delightful little room, which is all of glass, is cozily carpeted and furnished and the views from which 'cap the climax' of the lovely out-door pictures which abound..."

The whole house was finished in natural redwood and lighted with electricity. A stable "corresponding in general design and finish to the house," also was built.

A.M. Johnston was born in Ireland in 1834, came to the U.S. in 1855 and acquired citizenship in 1859. His early work was with a flour and grocery business in Buffalo, New York, but he moved to Rockford, Illinois, where he founded the A.M. Johnston Oatmeal Milling Company and made a fortune. He married in 1875 and had one son, Ed Johnston, well-known in Santa Cruz. A.M. Johnston lost his fortune, but made another after coming to California in 1885 and

*continued on page 97*

# Calvary

# Episcopal

# Church

### 538 Center Street,
### Santa Cruz

*This wood Victorian Gothic Revival building has been acclaimed an "architectural jewel." It was built in 1864 for approximately $4,000, following plans drawn up by Joseph Boston, who, it is said, designed his church after one in England. Of special note is Calvary's beautiful curved apse with its six stained glass windows. It is the oldest known church building in continuous use in California, and the first church in the State to receive a bronze plaque from the California Heritage Council. It also is the first building in Santa Cruz to receive such an award for its authentic and interesting architecture. James W. Lenhoff, president of the Council, presented the bronze plaque on June 16, 1972.*

The history of Calvary Episcopal Church of Santa Cruz is as turbulent as the waters of storm-tossed Monterey Bay. At the center of the early beginnings was a frail girl who had come to California from New York in search of health.

Eliza Bull found health, a husband and family, and founded the church. She also was the first woman to hold public office in Santa Cruz. Eliza came via steamship to San Francisco where a brother, Thomas Bull, was prominent in banking circles. In the following year, 1862, Eliza was married to Joseph Boston who also had lived in New York but had come west to start a mercantile store. He is best remembered by Santa Cruz historians as the owner-operator of Boston Tannery, in partnership with R.C. Kirby and Edmund Jones in 1855.

Eliza rapidly regained her health, became the busy mother of five children, the first local woman to serve as a public school trustee, a writer and a much-sought speaker. She also was determined that the struggling Episcopal Church group in Santa Cruz should have its own permanent home: she deeded the site.

The church had been meeting in various places, with its first service in May, 1862—the same month Eliza and Joseph were married. Their wedding is the first in the church register. Services were conducted in the Santa Cruz Courtroom, in Temperance Hall on the Mission Street hill, in an "old flea-infested schoolhouse recently vacated by the Methodists," in the new Methodist Church and in homes.

In 1864 the Episcopalians formed a new parish with Joseph Boston as secretary and the Rev. C.F. Loop as missionary rector. Articles of incorporation were filed, Joseph got busy on plans for the church building and the cornerstone was laid June 29, 1864. The first service in the new building (minus windows, altar and pulpit) was held January 8, 1865.

A continuing storm of financial problems beset the new church. Pews were rented out to help pay the rector's salary. In 1889 the rector received only $40 per month as salary and the church was struggling to pay that, plus back taxes. In 1878 for a time, the church went into the produce business, allowing Isaac Taylor to plant alfalfa and potatoes on church property, for one-half the crops. In the early 1890's a more businesslike system was set up with pledge envelopes and by 1902 pews were advertised as "Seats Free." However, the church did not really sail out of troubled financial waters until after World War II, when the Rev. Norman H. Snow took over to serve for 29 years. In 1957 the Rev. Alexander Anderson, present rector, took over and due to the efforts of these men the church enjoys solid financial footing today.

Calvary Episcopal's sanctuary was long recognized as an architectural gem, but no one did much about it until rumors began to fly that the Church would have to be demolished and a larger sanctuary built. Again, a woman came to the rescue. A small group headed by Ada Jane Leamy worked to save the historic structure. On June 16, 1972, Calvary Episcopal Church was presented with a plaque by the California Heritage Council, the first church in California to be so honored, also the first building in Santa Cruz County to receive the award for its architecture.

# Heiner-Bowen House

### 346 Church Street, Santa Cruz

*Stick Style with touches of Eastlake and, in its fishscale shingles, a reminder of Queen Anne, this is a fascinating old structure. When the City of Santa Cruz acquired it, the foundation was sound; it had been put on concrete piers a few years ago. The house, one of the city's earliest wood duplexes, was built in 1877 by two carpenters named Alexander and Marsh. Although originally estimated at $2,000, Messrs. Alexander and Marsh were able to build the ten-room redwood double tenement for $1,373. The bathrooms were remodeled slightly, but the kitchen was adequate and was not touched. Baseboard electric heat was also installed. The major construction change was a complete rewiring job. The City of Santa Cruz has demonstrated in this house what can be done with suitable older structures. It is interesting to note reactions: Office workers — "We like it!" General public: "It's interesting and fun to visit." Department head: "It's got a warm atmosphere for offices, and it's efficient too." One reminder: most of the work on the house was done by Parks and Recreation personnel, thus cutting down on remodeling and repair labor costs. Total cost for rehabilitation: $15,000.*

For $25,000, plus another $15,000 for remodeling, the City of Santa Cruz has acquired a handsome old house that was one of the city's first wood duplexes.

It is now restored and remodeled, and is in use as offices for Santa Cruz Department of City Parks and Recreation.

Not the least of the acquisition was the huge old redwood tree (*Sequoia sempervirens*) to the west of the house. Each year the tree "bursts into flame" when the bougainvillaea vine that climbs its height, blooms. The tree and the vine have been landmarks for years, and were written about by Santa Cruz oldtimer and historian, Ernest Otto, in many a column.

Heiner-Bowen House was built as a rental in 1877 by Mrs. Rosanna Bowen who also had a fine home built for herself on the adjacent corner — Chestnut and Locust Streets.

The "double tenement" house, which was the rental, cost $1,373 to build and contained ten rooms, was two stories high and boasted closets. Mrs. Bowen also lived in it for a number of years, according to a granddaughter, Mrs. Frank Wilson of Santa Cruz.

The house occupies the site of the former E. Kunitz Soap and Glue Factory. Mr. Kunitz had moved his factory out to River Street, then sold the property to Mrs. Bowen.

In May of 1970, pressed for space, although an addition to Santa Cruz City Hall had been built a few years ago, the City bought the old duplex for $25,000. The wall separating the two stairways was removed and a handsome rail and support post in the Victorian style were designed and made by Duncan McKenzie of the city parks crew. He also built and installed the counter for the main office, which was one of the living rooms. The other living room is now a conference room. One wall was added to create a bathroom; closets are now bookcases. Old clocks, an antique settee set and several rolltop desks were borrowed from Santa Cruz Museum. They are right at home in the old house. Wall to wall carpeting covers the floors; walls are papered in patterns appropriate to the Victorian era, and woodwork is painted corresponding colors in the various rooms.

The house contains the main downstairs office, conference room, lavatories and small kitchen. Upstairs there are four offices, bath and storage.

The house probably should be called Bowen House, because H.O. Heiner did not acquire it until about 1926. In that year he planted the redwood tree which is now about 100 feet tall. Heiner came to Santa Cruz from his native Redwood City in 1922 to take a position with Santa Cruz Land Title Company. When he died, age 80, in 1966, he was president of the firm. He and his wife, Inez Heiner, were known for their interest in animals, and he founded the Society for the Prevention of Cruelty to Animals facility at DeLaveaga Park.

Mrs. Heiner lived in the home at 346 Church Street until 1966 when she died.

Heiner-Bowen House was opened formally to the public on May 3, 1974, with an open house hosted by Paul Thiltgen, director of City Parks and Recreation.

PROD's first headquarters after and before rehabilitation.
Upper photo: Exterior view.
Left: Double stairway of house after wall was removed.
Lower right: The former living room now the main office of the Santa Cruz
City Parks and Recreation Department.

# PROD

### (Private Revitalization of Downtown)

Chuck Abbott and his wife Esther, both nationally-known photographers, came to Santa Cruz to retire in 1963. They planned to take it easy, except for their fall and spring auto trips to photograph scenery for national magazines.

Instead of taking it easy, they found several major projects that needed "doing" in Santa Cruz. Esther retained the photography work, making periodic trips. Chuck — no one ever called him anything else — stayed in Santa Cruz, rolled up his sleeves and pitched in.

First there was Pacific Avenue to do something about. Economically, the Avenue was hurting. Vacant stores...dwindling business as shoppers more and more patronized outlying shopping centers. The downtown was dying, many feared. Santa Cruz City had a population of 32,000 — and 22 empty stores along Pacific Avenue. The Avenue itself was too narrow for modern-day traffic; it dated back to ox-team days.

Chuck Abbott decided a Mall was the answer. He visited malls, successful and otherwise, all over the country, taking notes, making color slides, asking questions, learning. Esther went along and helped.

Together they showed slides and talked Mall until Santa Cruz' Pacific Garden Mall, a partial Mall, but a successful one, was a reality.

But the Mall wasn't enough. Chuck and Esther had purchased several older houses, refurbished and restored them, lived in one and rented out the other two. These weren't big fancy Victorians. They were the ordinary kind of house that average families occupied around the turn of the century. In "recycling" the older, less-desirable houses, the Abbotts actually started a "recycling" wave in their neighborhood with near neighbors painting up and fixing up and planting street trees. Their block on Lincoln Street took on a more pleasant aura. But just a few doors away, on the same street, there were rundown houses that challenged Chuck. In fact there was a whole row of look-alike flats, paint peeling, porches sagging, postage-stamp front yards with weeds thriving.

Once these flats had been handsome. Chuck felt they could be again. After months of work and planning and negotiations, PROD was born. And Chuck became what he jokingly referred to as "a victim of the rehabilitation bug."

The Abbotts acquired the row of flats and put a crew of eager college students to work in their spare time. Tons of trash were removed, porches were repaired, interiors were renovated, painted, re-wired. The flats were painted a soft green with brick trim and the tiny front yards were paved with used bricks and planted with trees and ivy. The flats were rented to students who raise their own vegetables in the large backyard which runs through the center of the block.

What makes PROD important is that it is done with private money; this allows greater leeway. PROD also makes use of job trainees — students and part-time workers who are under the supervision of retired, skilled craftsmen. The trainees are not used for new construction but are available for restoration and repair work.

*Chuck Abbott*

*continued on page 98*

# Santa Cruz YWCA

303 Walnut Avenue,
Santa Cruz

*The main YWCA building in Santa Cruz looks as if it should be located in some European town, rather than rubbing elbows with the Victorians which surround it on three sides. When the Salvator Fachutars built it as their studio-home in 1921-22, they ignored past and present Santa Cruz architectural trends and chose a plain two-story box-like structure with hip roof and small-paned windows. They also placed it almost on the sidewalks of two sides, and had a wire fence constructed between it and passers-by. It's a curious building, attractive in an unusual way, perhaps for its purity of line.*

*The newly acquired Victorian, at 315 Walnut Avenue, is a combination of Eastlake and Queen Anne, with fishscale shingles. The YWCA intends to retain its Victorian atmosphere.*

Along with glue and soap factories, Santa Cruz had at one time a perfume factory. Today it's the Santa Cruz Young Woman's Christian Association headquarters.

Besides being a perfume factory, the building was said to be the "largest music house between San Francisco and Los Angeles, and the only one in Santa Cruz handling all sheet music and musical literature in addition to all varieties of perfumes and lovely perfume bottles."

This all came about in 1921 when Mr. and Mrs. Salvator P. Fachutar came to Santa Cruz to build a studio-home. They built it at what was then 115 Walnut Avenue, on the southwest corner of Walnut and Chestnut.

S.P. Fachutar was a violin-maker and composer as well as a perfume chemist. An old photograph shows him looking prim and proper, the tips of his white shirt collar folded back in neat triangles, a small flower in his buttonhole, dark suit, eyeglasses with gold rims and a dove gray derby-type hat on his head.

Two years before he died, on Sunday, August 15, 1937, a Southern Pacific Club Band Concert honored Fachutar by playing five of his compositions: "Marcha Espanola," "Dulce Cares," "Waltz Springtime," "Intermezzo" and "March Southern Pacific." This band concert no doubt took place at Santa Cruz Beach Bandstand.

After Mr. Fachutar died in 1939, his widow continued to live on in the studio-home. She was something of a celebrity in her own right, Frances Bagnell Fachutar. She continued her husband's projects of helping young musicians financially, and when her wealthy brother, Benjamin Bagnell, died in Milwaukee, she had many of his art treasures shipped out to her Santa Cruz home.

In 1944, Mrs. Fachutar, in failing health, sold her home and property to the Santa Cruz YWCA which had been a part of the Monterey YWCA District until 1942. Instrumental in the changes and the purchase were Mrs. Fred (Mayte) McPherson, a past district president; Edith Hinds, Mabel Byrne, Bertha Adams, Laura Stanley and Jennie Richardson.

With the Fachutar studio-home, the eager Y women got a large garden in which grew the roses and other flowers from which Mr. Fachutar had distilled his perfumes.

For years the YWCA was comfortably housed in the structure but recently, faced with growing pains, the Y acquired the combination Eastlake and Queen Anne house next door at 315 Walnut. The title search revealed that the property goes back as part of a 16 acre parcel belonging to James Williams and heirs in 1866. It was sold to Frederick A. Hihn in 1867, to Julia Johnston in 1905, to James and George O'Brien in 1910, to Anne Hambrook in 1921 and to Arthur Eastman in 1929. Wilbur Schultz bought it in 1941, Lora and Mabel Jameson in 1944, then Roy Austin, Kidwards, Holsers, Roys, Weltys and Schroeders owned it briefly, one by one. In 1973 the YWCA bought it.

The house was probably built in 1892-95. It was once used as a photography studio by Roy Austin, and later as an apartment house.

Instrumental in the purchase of these houses for the YWCA were Blanche Clark, Mrs. Norman Sullivan, Mrs. James Burt, Mrs. Sam

*continued on page 98*

78

# Sadler House

### 123 Green Street,
### Santa Cruz

*A two-story Italianate house built circa 1870. Original "core" of the house was the box-like first Methodist Church of Santa Cruz, built in 1850.*

To look at the handsome old house today, one would never suspect its humble beginnings.

Up the street from it, on the southeast corner of Green and Mission Streets, the Methodists constructed their first church, a plain wood building 30 by 20 feet, built in 1850. It served until 1864 when a new sanctuary was put up.

Eager to pay off their $4,000 debt on the new church building, church trustees decided to sell off part of the church property of seven acres. They sold a row of lots along what became the west side of Green Street to a young man who had just acquired a bride and was eager to turn a dollar or two. Otis Longley bought the property. He didn't have long to wait for another customer for part of his land. William J. Reynolds had just married Mary Simpson and they needed a home. Reynolds plunked down $125 for a lot from Otis, then he bargained with the church fathers for the old "box" church building.

Reynolds bought the discarded church building and moved it down Green Street to his lot and added rooms onto it. Three years after establishing his "church home" there, Reynolds sold the house and land for $6,000 to James Dougherty, a Santa Clara Valley lumberman.

The next owner was T.W. Kelly who also did some remodeling. Kelly ran the "Racket Store" on Pacific Avenue, an early version of the 10-cent store.

In 1920 Professor D.C. Clark bought the house. Clark was Santa Cruz City Schools Superintendent. When he died, the fine old house, which had been greatly embellished through the years, passed to his daughter, Mrs. Don Sadler. Mrs. Sadler's daughters sold it in 1964 and it was acquired by Mr. and Mrs. Edward Tunheim who cherish it today.

Mr. Tunheim has gone underneath the house and established the location of its oldest portion — the Methodist "box." Nearly 125 years old, the portion is still sound, its virgin redwood intact.

Old accounts state that the "box" was built with local lumber furnished by one John D. Green who lived nearby. Green Street itself originally was casually referred to as "the church street," and didn't get its name of Green Street until the 1860's. It supposedly is named for John D. Green. Only one block long, Green Street originally was the main thoroughfare between Santa Cruz downtown, and the Potrero — or pasture area — north of town off River Street.

123 GREEN STREET

# Triplett House

## 240 Walnut Avenue, Santa Cruz

*This small architectural jewel is about 100 years old and was built, along with its twin next door, by W.A. Reese, according to the present owners, Barbara and Ed Rosso. The Rossos found a piece of an old building record when they were restoring the house. Over the years, the street number changed from 96 Walnut Avenue to 98, then finally to 240 Walnut. In the days when Victorian society was in full pompous tread in Santa Cruz, Walnut Avenue was the address to have. The house has seven rooms, a small tower, curving front porch, fancy shingles and spindles, and is Queen Anne style. It is one of two identical structures, side by side.*

For more than 30 years, every woman in Santa Cruz County who went into Leask's Department Store in Santa Cruz for gloves or ribbons, was acquainted with Anita Triplett.

Ladies wore gloves — and ribbons — in those days. Anita, a frail little old maid, would rest their elbows on a small velvet cushion on the counter top, then gently, so gently, ease the tight new gloves onto their fingers one by one, and down over their hands.

When I knew her she was gray-haired and I thought she must be terribly old. Four generations of my family had traded at Leask's, and my grandmother belonged to the same Santa Cruz Parlor, Native Daughters of the Golden West, that Anita belonged to. So we knew her quite well. She was always sweet, always cheerful, a hard worker — and completely dominated by an older sister, Pearl.

Once I telephoned Nita, as she was always called, to ask if I could write a small story about her historic family background. Nita halfway agreed to let me do it, when, in the background, Pearl's voice came over the wire loud and firm: "No publicity! No! Tell her absolutely not!" And that was that.

It wasn't personal — that I knew. It was just that Pearl loathed publicity with an undying vigor that never left her to the day she died.

Actually, the Triplett sisters (there were four) had fine old Spanish blood in their veins, but they seldom, if ever, mentioned it. Their grandparents were Simon and Petra Perez, who were married in 1849 at Santa Cruz Mission. Petra was from the well-to-do Gonzales family. The Perez family owned much of the area at the eastern edge of Santa Cruz and where Dominican Hospital is located today. Simon and Petra had ten children, among whom was a daughter Josephine, and a son, James. Josephine was baptized in the old Santa Cruz Mission, attended school there, grew up and married Remus Triplett. He was a member of prominent families of Kentucky and Virginia. Josephine and Remus had four daughters: Anita (Nita), Pearl, Josephine and Mabel.

James Perez, uncle to the girls, attended Chestnutwood's Business College in Santa Cruz, secured a position with Wells Fargo and went to El Paso, Texas, and Chihuahua, Mexico, for that firm. In an 1889 letter to his mother, he wrote: "...went to bed in Arizona and got up in New Mexico and ate my dinner in Texas and I will get my breakfast in Old Mexico." James had been highly recommended for the position with Wells Fargo. No less than W.H. Bias, County Treasurer of Santa Cruz, had written in his spidery hand: "James F. Perez: A promising young man, born, raised and educated in this place. Has filled several positions, where business energy and honesty has crowned him with respect and confidence in every instance. And I cheerfully recommend him to any position he may deem himself qualified to fill. Very truly Yours, W.H. Bias."

The Perez family adobe home was located at Paul Sweet Lane, but Anita, Pearl and Mabel bought a small but elegant house on Walnut Avenue in Santa Cruz in 1945, and it was their home until they died, one by one. Their mother, Josephine Triplett, was widowed in 1912 and died in 1931. Her brother and sister, Simon and Mollie Perez, lived in the family adobe until the late 1940's, old, proud, land-poor

*continued on page 99*

Hulda McLean 1974

# Dake House

### 410 High Street, Santa Cruz

*So tall are the trees and shrubs around this house that it can hardly be seen from High Street, which is directly below it at a much lower level. The house is located on a large lot against the hill, above the street, and is reached by a long flight of steps which cut up through the fine limestone wall that fronts the property. A winding driveway curves up behind the house to the garage. This photograph, taken by Pete Amos, shows only the second story of the house; the first is completely hidden by the shrubbery. Main entry is directly beneath the second floor balcony railing. Every window on this, the south side of the house, has a sweeping view of Santa Cruz and Monterey Bay — that is, if the shrubs were trimmed a bit! The house is redwood with a full concrete basement and full attic — really four stories.*

High on a bank above High Street, flanked by two old palm trees and almost hidden behind shrubs, is Dake House.

The retaining wall that bounds the property, rising from the street level to the garden level, is an interesting part of old Santa Cruz itself, being constructed of limestone chunks, as are several of the town's oldest stone walls.

The house, originally a handsome Colonial Revival, has been slightly changed in appearance in recent years, with the addition of enclosed areas on the front porch which was open when built.

It was constructed about 1900 by Mr. and Mrs. Lawrence J. Dake as their home, and remained in the Dake family as the home of the eldest son, Clarence G. Dake, until 1933.

Lawrence Dake was born in New York City, March 24, 1858, and came to Santa Cruz from Milwaukee in 1876. He had, at age 14, been employed in Milwaukee in the business offices of the Northwestern Mutual Life Insurance Company and also as a clerk in Bradstreet's Commercial Agency.

In Santa Cruz he worked for Thomas Wright, managed a flour mill and kept books. When things slowed down he went to San Francisco where he was bookkeeper for R.D. Hume and Co., commission merchants. From there he traveled to Tulare County and was briefly in the business of raising sheep — although it is something of a mystery to his descendants as to why he did that when he so obviously was a man of the business office world.

In 1883 he was again in Santa Cruz and began studying the Pitman system of shorthand with a view to passing the examination for court reporter. In nine months he was doing 150 words per minute — and the position of Supreme Court reporter was his. In 1884 in partnership with his brother-in-law, George Chittenden, he established the California Market, and after several years he went into the Land Title business with H.E. Makinney, later taking it over completely. His son, Clarence G. Dake, followed him in the land title business and today has offices in Monterey and Salinas.

In 1885 Lawrence was married to Clara Chittenden. They had four children, two daughters who died as children, and two sons, Clarence, already mentioned, and Irving Dake. Lawrence Dake also was elected chairman of the Republican County Central Committee.

His home on High Street was a comfortable and large house in a day when large houses were the general rule. The front stair led up from an entry hall that was a room in itself with fireplace and windows overlooking the city. A back stair served for the hired help and took off from the back hall which ran the length of the house. The dining room and entry hall fireplaces were corner ones, the large living room had a larger fireplace on its west wall. There was a basement and a full attic — and five large bedrooms on the second floor — all but one with glorious views out over the city and Monterey Bay.

The senior Dakes were active in Methodist Church circles where Clara sang, and they entertained often in their home. In later years, Clarence and his wife, Callista Martin Dake, entertained her sister Omega Nu sorority members and his fellow fraternity brothers, the GEKs, at parties there. The Clarence Dakes also started raising their family of four children in the big house. It was a great house for children and parties.

# Section IV

# Out of Town. . .

# The Little White Church

Soquel

Ships' carpenters of the early days in California knew their trade and they built well. They had to. Shoddy work could send ships — and the men who sailed them — fathoms deep to Davey Jones' Locker.

One ship's carpenter, home from the seas and the shipyards, took hammer and saw in hand to construct Soquel's "Little White Church in the Vale."

S.A. Hall was a rugged seaman with a firm jaw and a stern forehead. He had learned his trade in Maine, a state of hardy seamen and adventurers. In 1870 in Soquel, Hall began the task of building a suitable house of worship for Soquel Congregationalists who had been meeting for four years in a blacksmith shop.

Hall envisioned a New England-type church like the ones in Maine where he grew up. He drew his plans, perhaps working on a sheet of coarse brown paper with a stubby pencil. Then he headed the volunteer work crews who put up the church. The lot on which it was built was a gift from Joshua Parrish, Soquel pioneer, in a day when land around Soquel was valued at $14.22 per acre. Soquel families — a handful of them — raised the $2,700 the church cost. It was dedicated August 7, 1870.

The Soquel church grew slowly in a settlement that was located four miles from Santa Cruz, reached by horse and wagon or buggy, over roads that were dusty tracks in summer, muddy bogs in winter. Soquel was a roistering little lumber town. Stage coaches lumbered through, passing from Santa Cruz to San Juan Bautista, stopping at Aptos and Watsonville briefly on their way. Above a welter of dust, mud, snapping whips, laboring oxen and horse teams hauling lumber, rowdy teamsters and woodsmen on weekend sprees, the Soquel church stood like an oasis with its New England spire pointing to the heavens. The spire was 60 feet tall; the 1,000-pound bell was placed in it in 1877 by the Rev. A.C. Duncan.

Names on the early church register echo the history of the Soquel area — Porter, Noble, Grover, Mattison, Hames, Daubenbiss — people who built the town, the school, founded the Ladies' Aid Society and brought law and order into that rough pioneer day.

Over the years a few changes were necessary. In 1893 the church was moved 20 feet and a choir alcove was added; in 1903 the kerosene lamps were replaced with a carbide lighting plant; in 1905 the social hall was built and a year later, $76 was spent for a shed to protect the horses that drew the buggies and wagons of church-goers.

In 1925 the church starred as the background for a movie, "Johnstown Flood," in which Janet Gaynor was featured as the tragic bride who was swept away during her wedding ceremony.

In 1943 the chancel was rebuilt — after all, it was getting along in years. A set of 21 chimes was installed in 1954. Ten years went by uneventfully but in 1964 the church fathers realized that more extensive work was needed on the sanctuary. The steeple spire was in danger of collapsing due to rot and termites. New flooring was necessary, wiring, and a foundation under the entire structure. Everybody got busy — about $25,000 was needed. There were church suppers, rummage sales and many donations. The work was done and a fresh coat of white paint added the final touch.

*continued on page 99*

# The Bay View Hotel

## Aptos

*Built about 1870 by Jose Arano, the hotel is Italianate with French mansard roof, a style popular in the 1860's to 1880's. The roof and third floor were added in 1883. Porches, once open, have been closed for use as dining areas.*

Mention "Aptos" and immediately a picture of the old Bay View Hotel flashes into one's mind. It sits stately but comfortably, behind a huge magnolia tree, a picture page out of Santa Cruz County's past.

The hotel was built about 1870 by Jose Arano, a French immigrant who married the youngest daughter of Don Rafael Castro who owned the 6,680-acre Rancho Aptos. The Rancho had been granted to Don Castro in 1833.

The hotel was two stories originally, and it housed Arano's grocery store and the Aptos Post Office for a time. Under Arano's proprietorship it became famous for its Spanish food. He doubled in brass, as the saying goes, and became Aptos' first postmaster as well as its hotel-keeper and grocer. It is said that when the hotel was under construction, Arano personally inspected every bit of lumber that went into it. He also selected every stick of furniture for the hotel, most of which is there today. The four handsome marble fireplaces on the main floor are originals. In 1883 the third floor was added.

For more than 40 years the Bay View was a popular watering place for wealthy and prominent people and its guests included Lillian Russell and King Kalakaua of Hawaii at various times. When Claus Spreckels, the sugar beet king, bought a large part of Rancho Aptos, he brought many famous visitors to Aptos.

The hotel was a busy place when the Loma Prieta Lumber Company was running full blast in the hills behind it. F.A. Hihn's Valencia Mill also shipped from Aptos and busiest years were from 1880 to 1900. However, the great redwood trees in the hills were finally logged out, railroad activity was curtailed and shortly before World War I the hotel closed.

In 1944 Fred W. Toney and his wife Elma bought the old building. A service wing had burned in 1929 but the main structure was intact. In spite of warnings by professional house movers that "it couldn't be done," Toney and a crew of Aptos men placed timbers and rollers beneath the old building and moved it about 100 feet to its present location. It formerly stood at the corner of Trout Gulch Road, nearer the railroad tracks.

Fred and Elma ran the Bay View as a hotel and eating place until 1972, and Elma also sold copies of antiques on the side. The Toneys still own the historic structure but now lease it out to Frank Leal and Pete Marchese, who operate it as a hotel, restaurant and bar.

In the past few years the hotel has been the scene of the annual doings of the Aptos Ladies Tuesday Afternoon Society — *and* their battle with the Southern Pacific Railroad. The Ladies planted shrubs along the railroad right-of-way in an effort to beautify the Village of Aptos. The railroad protested. The Ladies stood firm. In fact they threatened to lie down on the railroad tracks in physical protest. The railroad gave in, and things have been quiet ever since.

# His Home Was His Castle

Ben Lomond

*This miniature stone castle on the banks of the San Lorenzo River in Ben Lomond has been referred to as a "delightful architectural folly." It is located on the northern edge of Ben Lomond, southwest side of Highway 9, just before crossing the river, traveling north. It was built of stones gathered out of the river bed, and is open to tours on weekends.*

Robert Howden's Ben Lomond home was his castle, and his stone castle was his home.

He called himself an "everyday Scotsman," but his one burning desire was to live in a castle. He did. He built it himself. Howden selected a beautiful bend on the San Lorenzo River in Ben Lomond, a San Lorenzo Valley town where he had spent vacations camping in a tent. There, in the early 1920's, with local hired help, Howden built his castle. And he patterned it after Scottish castles he remembered from his boyhood days in Scotland.

The Ben Lomond castle went together slowly, although it was to be much smaller than its Scottish counterparts. Every stone was hand-picked and hand set. Howden's regular home and business were located in Oakland where he operated a factory that manufactured all kinds of tiles. But Howden's heart was in the "highlands" of Ben Lomond and he even wrote poems about it in his spare time.

In 1922 he wrote: "Ben Lomond, nestling 'mong the heights, Above fair Santa Cruz, Your peaceful quiet my soul delights, Your charm awakes my muse..."

"I love the music of your stream, Along its winding ways, While on its face the pale moon beams, Makes dazzling, dancing rays..."

In a 1931 poem, Howden wrote after a hard day's work lifting stones: "A day of usefulness I've learned, Is honest work to pleasure turned..."

Apparently all Ben Lomondites were not in accord with Howden and his ideas, because in the same poem, one line states: "Crazy they thought me to thus embark, And build on such a site; 'Tis a foolish scheme, was the one remark, To be heard on every side..."

The castle was completed in 1926. Howden, who spent his early life in Scotland as a stone carver, used his talent to etch the panes of the glass windows in his castle. They depict Scottish scenes and the poems of Sir Walter Scott and Robert Burns. It had only three rooms when he completed it.

Howden kept his castle until 1937 when he sold it to Dr. and Mrs. Norman Sullivan of Santa Cruz who enlarged it and modernized a bit. Since then it has changed hands four times and each new owner has added to its comfort and charm without changing the basic appearance. Many rooms were added by the Weatherlys.

Today it contains about 15 rooms, some of them quite small, according to Mrs. Ivy Lee Weatherly who owns it and lives there with her flock of 12 cats. She opens the castle for tours on Saturdays, Sundays and holidays.

"It takes me about five hours to ready it for a tour," she said in reference to its many rooms. "Other castles have bats and rats — but mine has cats."

## THE HIHN MANSION

*continued from page 4*

After a long and busy life. F.A. Hihn died on August 23, 1913. Ten years later, almost to the day, on August 22, 1923, the Hihn heirs deeded the family mansion to the City of Santa Cruz. The City accepted the deed officially on December 6, 1923, by vote of the City Council.

There is some evidence that the structure was used as a City Hall from 1920, three years before it was formally deeded. This is probably correct, as purchase negotiations took place over a long period of time, according to Attorney Donald Younger, a grandson of F.A. Hihn.

F.A. Hihn's wife, Therese, lived in the huge old home until her death on April 20, 1919. And grandson Younger was born in the house while his father, Charles B. Younger, was on a fishing trip to Waddell Creek. The date was May 16, 1903.

The magnificent old house, with its glass-roofed conservatory, was used by the City from about 1920 to 1937 when it was torn down to make way for Santa Cruz' new City Hall. The Hihn gardens contained such rare and fine plantings that many of them were saved and re-planted at the Golden Gate International Exposition on Treasure Island, San Francisco Bay, in 1939.

There are few people around today who remember that Peter Thrift was the Hihn gardener — or that there was a skating rink in the attic of the Hihn home and the kids were supplied with wooden-wheeled skates.

## RENNIE HOUSE

*continued from page 8*

Today only an ancient Cypress tree marks the site of his house.

The three-story house cost $4,000 when Rennie had it built in 1890. Much of the interior woodwork was the finest redwood, cut and milled in Santa Cruz County.

## HOTALING BUILDING

*continued from page 14*

Hinkle lived to a venerable old age, became a vice president of the Bank of Italy (Bank of America today), president of Santa Cruz Chamber of Commerce, a school board member and Mayor of Santa Cruz. He died in 1959.

His store is unique in that its architecture has not been tampered with much since it was built.

For years the Arlington Hotel, really a rooming house, was operated upstairs. It was a genteel establishment where those low on cash could sneak down to Hinkle's, spend a few pennies for bananas, bread, coffee and a can of canned heat to do a bit of surreptitious cooking upstairs in their rooms.

The building's odd, cock-eyed stance repeats the angle at which Mission Street joined Pacific when horses and wagons plodded past in hock-deep mud or dust, depending on the season.

Hotaling, builder of this controversial structure, seems to have had a talent for troublesome buildings. One of his structures in San Francisco was a whiskey warehouse that survived the earthquake

**HOTALING BUILDING**

and fire of 1906 — much to the dismay of certain citizens. Charles K. Field wrote this quatrain, which was widely quoted in the San Francisco Bay area: "If, as they say, God spanked the town for being over-frisky, Why did he burn the churches down — and save Hotaling's whiskey?"

**HAGEMANN HOUSE**

*continued from page 18*

Harbor and Twin Lakes Beach, if properly planned.

And what of Hagemann House with its twin towers and ornate trim?

"We would like to see it preserved as the original homestead," he says.

**THE COUNTESS' LOG CABIN**

*continued from page 24*

owner is a retired lecturer from University of California at Santa Cruz.

She takes a delight in the cabin's historic setting, although the old mill wheel across the way is gone. She rescued the ironwork and the garden terraces, and she is once again building the log cabin's reputation for hospitality and fine food. Today it's the Babbling Brook Restaurant.

**CLIFF CREST**

*continued from page 32*

The Jeters had no children, and when Jennie Jeter died in 1959, a niece inherited the house. It passed out of the family in 1968 and has been modernized — but not essentially changed — since then, by Peter Haan.

**THE WILLEY HOME**

*continued from page 36*

Two little girls who used to play in the big attic, Ruth and Margaret Willey, daughters of Henry and Frances, grew up in the house and were married there, after graduation from "Uncle Samuel's College" in Berkeley. They stood in their bridal gowns, in the big bay window, under homemade garlands of leaves and flowers, then left for their new homes as rice cascaded down the broad front steps of Willey House.

Today they treasure these memories of the big house at the corner of Mission and Sylvar — Mrs. Ruth Snook, and Mrs. Margaret Millbank. Mrs. Millbank has gathered the family history into a charming little booklet, privately printed.

**HALSEY HOUSE**

*continued from page 40*

Then in 1961, after years of teaching and correcting papers, then retiring to take walks and live quietly and drink tea in a world that

## HALSEY HOUSE

was changing in such frightening ways, the sisters died. Clara went first, in January. Alice lived until July. And the big tall white house with the tower was empty at last.

## BALDWIN HOUSE

continued from page 50

Neighbors included Baldwin cousins up the street at 445 Locust, and several houses away, H.E. Irish. Ruth's father, Amos, was associated in business with Mr. Irish and ran the piano department in Irish's music and stationery store.

Ruth's father, mother and grandmother all died in the family home.

And today Ruth walks wonderingly through the garden, thinking of the years that have passed and the living that took place in the house.

"See that huge pine tree? My mother planted it. That palm tree? She started it from a date pit. I lost one of her trees out by the front walk a year or so ago. I hated to see it die," she added sadly.

Baldwin roots go deep.

## HOLLINS HOUSE

continued from page 58

*Upper: Babe Didrikson Zaharias [l.] and Marion Hollins with golf partners. Lower: The famous golfer of that era, Bobby Jones, at Pasatiempo.*

dominant 'place in the sun' as the rendezvous of the Western Riviera as well as the relaxation resort of many of Hollywood's most famous and glamorous stars..." So went an article of the day.

Word got around that the Pasatiempo Estates Company had acquired 600 feet of prime beach frontage on Monterey Bay where a beach club was to be constructed. All this despite the great depression! Marion Hollins was appointed to serve as the first woman member of Santa Cruz Chamber of Commerce. A financial genius, everyone assumed. What they didn't know was that this remarkable woman was digging to the bottom of her purse which had held two and one-half million dollars to start with.

In December, 1938, the bubble burst, her company's capital was exhausted and the sale of Pasatiempo was announced. The beach property went first. The Golf and Country Club were sold to C.F. Baker of New York, and several partners. On November 4, 1940, Marion left Pasatiempo, and a sad day it was. Pasatiempo had been sold again — to P.M. Lansdale. In January, 1941, the golf course closed down; no one was playing golf. The depression was in full swing. The beautiful Clubhouse became the home of Mr. Lansdale, then in 1952 it became the home of the Tanner Wilsons.

Marion Hollins went back to work again, at Del Monte in Monterey, across the Bay from her dream development. Her dreams had come true for awhile, even though they finally crashed into financial ruin on the old Carbonero Rancho. She was sick for about three weeks in a Pacific Grove hospital before she died in 1944.

Today her Clubhouse is known as Hollins House and is the scene of weddings, receptions, luncheons, cocktail parties and other festive affairs, as part of the now-thriving Pasatiempo Golf Club.

Marion herself was a plain and practical (except with money) woman who wore long, unbecoming skirts and baggy sweaters. She disliked being photographed and few pictures of her exist. She

## HOLLINS HOUSE

played top-notch golf, loved horses, had a reverence for trees, spent her last cent to create beauty, and died a pauper. Was she ever bitter?

"Never," says a woman who had worked with her for years. "Never!"

## PALAIS MONTE CARLO

continued from page 64

The California Heritage Council's Certificate of Recognition is presented Mrs. Pat Wilkinson for her restoration of Palais Monte Carlo. Mr. and Mrs. James Lenhoff are presenting the certificate at "Patty's Palace."

The house was mortgaged, and had to be sold. It was about all that was left of the Major's fortune. It changed hands for a few years — until 1967, when a woman who had fallen in love with it as a child, was able to acquire it. Patricia Sambuck Wilkinson had been in the house when she was a small girl, with her grandmother, Mrs. Stephen Scurich of Watsonville. Pat had kept an eye on the mansion for years — and finally, one day, it was hers.

She spent months in a labor of love, restoring, cleaning, painting, searching for the right pieces of furniture for the house. She treasures the priceless stained glass windows — the elephant hide that lines the former dining room — the elegant staircase, the onyx fireplace and the gold-plated lighting fixtures.

Palais Monte Carlo — or Patty's Palace as it is now sometimes called — is apartments today and she lives in one of them. The house has been awarded the California Heritage Council's Certificate of Recognition.

The old mansion has come into its own — a far cry from the sad day when Mr. Jeter found the Major's last request — a note that said, "Please do me one last favor and chloroform our poor old cat."

## COOPER HOUSE

continued from page 66

fought their battles with society.

When the 1867 structure burned in 1894, Cooper House was built — but prices had gone up. It cost $53,475. The year was 1895. Originally it had an imposing and slightly out-of-scale tower, but the earthquake of 1906 damaged it and it was removed.

Today, under Max Walden's direction, there are boutique shops and a bar on the first and second floors and a restaurant and liquor store in the basement, which boasts fascinating arched brick ceilings. There is also an outdoor sidewalk cafe in good weather, and a music combo plays there for the enjoyment of all — the lunching public and passers-by. Sometimes there is someone dancing, or a mime show...whatever, it is a sign of the changing scene in Santa Cruz. One wonders what the Cooper brothers would say now.

## JOHNSTON HOUSE

continued from page 70

establishing a grain, feed and flour business in Santa Cruz on the corner of Pacific Avenue and Soquel, where the Bank of America is today. He died in 1901 and his widow sold the big house to Arthur B. Cotton in 1909, according to Lee Johnston, wife of a grandson, the late Dr. Malcolm Johnston.

**JOHNSTON HOUSE**

A.M. Johnston's son, Ed Johnston, graduated from Santa Cruz High School with the Class of 1896 and went on to the University of California at Berkeley. After his father died, Ed disposed of the feed and grain business and went into the electrical business in which he was vastly more interested, forming a partnership with Frank Carroll.

The old house somewhere along through the years lost its finial "topknot" from its tower. It changed hands a number of times, serving as home to the Dan Hurts for perhaps the longest period, 1955 to 1971. With the exception of kitchen and bathrooms and a second floor gallery on the rear, the house is essentially as it was when originally constructed.

Today it is owned by Mr. and Mrs. Leland Zeidler who are dedicated to its preservation. One unusual note is the restored gazebo in the front yard which was in complete disrepair, due to the passing of the years. It was restored with "old materials" rescued from other venerable Santa Cruz buildings that were demolished.

**PROD**

continued from page 76

*PROD's Queen Anne flats.*

Chuck Abbott's PROD program gained nation-wide attention and was awarded a grant by HUD (Department of Housing and Urban Development) to make its philosophy known, nation-wide, through printed brochures and pictures. It's easy to take a stately Victorian and do something spectacular with it. It's not easy to take run-down, ordinary old houses and make them into something attractive that can be rented out at average rental prices to average people. Not everyone can live in a mansion.

It's also not an easy project to upgrade the less desirable neighborhoods — but Chuck and Esther Abbott showed how it can be done in an economically feasible way.

At the same time, young people were put to work learning a skill.

Chuck was 70 years old when he first came to Santa Cruz. He died in December, 1973, age 80, secure in the knowledge that PROD will live and grow. A Board of Directors is seeing to that. And in April, 1974, announcement was made of the Chuck Abbott Humanitarian Award, to be given by Friends of Santa Cruz Dominican Hospital to "someone who has improved the quality of community life in an on-going way." As Chuck Abbott did.

**SANTA CRUZ YWCA**

continued from page 78

Binsacca, Mrs. Harvey Edmund, Mrs. M.C. Hall, Mrs. Charles Brunjes, Mrs. Marion Shenk, Mrs. Albert Hoke, Mrs. Ada Jane Leamy, Mrs. Ora Stoodley, Mrs. Harold Gillette, Mrs. George Vanderbeek, Mrs. Charles Campbell, Texla Haas, Helen Caulkins, Caddie Cook, Aimee Hinds, Mary Frances Irelan, Mrs. Phil Harry, Mrs. John Bowen and Executive Director Agnes Gory.

Hard workers — and determined women, all of them!

**TRIPLETT HOUSE**

*continued from page 82*

and in failing health, according to a newspaper article of 1947 — "...the last vestige of the proud Perez family who knew and comprised the core of the gay Spanish times in early California..."

Of the four Triplett sisters, Josephine married and had a son; Mabel, Anita and Pearl remained maiden ladies, devout members of Holy Cross Church, leading quiet lives with only Anita venturing into the business world.

One by one they died. Josephine, then Anita, then Mabel; and last to go, Pearl of the firm convictions and outspoken manner. She had sold the little house to Mr. and Mrs. Ed Rosso and moved into an apartment, just a couple of years before she died on November 27, 1972. When she moved, she burned old pictures and documents, neighbors said, an idea that causes historians to weep, just thinking about it. But that's the way Pearl was. So different from Anita. And when Anita died, the whole world had turned upside down. Hardly anyone wore gloves anymore — even ladies.

**SOQUEL'S LITTLE WHITE CHURCH**

*continued from page 88*

A few months later, a fire broke out in the steeple and the entire town of Soquel, agnostics and church-goers alike, waited anxiously while it was brought under control.

Soquel's Little White Church has been photographed by shutter bugs, painted by artists and admired by almost everyone. In a way, it IS Soquel.

# Bibliography

*A Guide to Architecture in San Francisco and Northern California,* Peregrine Smith, Inc.

Bernhardi, Robert, *The Buildings of Berkeley,* 1971.

Department of Parks and Recreation, State of California, The Resources Agency, *Procedural Guide, Historic Resources Inventory.*

Guinn, Prof. J.M.* *History of the State of California and Biographical Record of Santa Cruz, San Benito, Monterey and San Luis Obispo Counties,* Chapman Pub. Co., 1903.

Harrison, E.S.* *History of Santa Cruz County,* Pacific Press, 1892.

Koch, Margaret, *Santa Cruz County — Parade of the Past,* Valley Publishers, Fresno, 1973.

Maass, John, *The Victorian Home in America,* Hawthorn Books, Inc., 1972.

*Procedural Guide, Historic Resources Inventory,* Department of Parks and Recreation, State of California, The Resources Agency.

Rowland, Leon, *Annals of Santa Cruz,* 1947.

### Newspapers, Periodicals, Documents

*Riptide,* published in Santa Cruz, Clifford N. Kilfoyl, publisher.

*Santa Cruz Sentinel* Newspaper, Jack Banks, publisher.

*Santa Cruz Surf* Newspaper.

Files of Santa Cruz Public Library.